"CHRYSOSTOM"

ST JOHN CHRYSOSTOM
ON MARRIAGE
AND
FAMILY LIFE

ST JOHN CHRYSOSTOM

ON MARRIAGE
AND
FAMILY LIFE

Translated by
Catharine P. Roth and David Anderson

Introduction by
Catharine P. Roth

ST VLADIMIR'S SEMINARY PRESS
CRESTWOOD, NEW YORK 10707
1986

This publication was made possible
through the generosity of

THE LOIS GEHA MEMORIAL
PUBLICATION FUND

Library of Congress Cataloging in Publication Data

John Chrysostom, Saint, d. 407.
  On marriage and family life.

  English and Greek.
  1. Marriage—Biblical teaching—Sermons. 2. Family—
Religious life—Biblical teaching—Sermons. 3. Bible.
N.T. Epistles of Paul—Sermons. 4. Marriage—Religious
aspects—Orthodox Eastern Church—Sermons. 5. Fam-
ily—Religious life—Orthodox Eastern Church—Sermons.
6. Orthodox Eastern Church—Doctrines—Sermons.
I. Roth, Catharine P. II. Anderson, David, 1953
III. Title.
BR65.C43E5   248.4   86-6756
ISBN 0-913836-86-9

Translation © 1986
Second Printing 1991

ST VLADIMIR'S SEMINARY PRESS

ISBN 0-913836-86-9

PRINTED IN THE UNITED STATES OF AMERICA
BY
J&J PRINTING, INC.
SYRACUSE, NY

Table of Contents

Introduction

The fourth century of the Christian era presented great challenges and opportunities for the Christian Church. The Emperor Constantine, in first legalizing Christianity and then establishing it as the state religion, marked a new stage in the progress of the Church from a small Jewish sect to the predominant faith of the Roman Empire. The Church was forced by its confrontation with pagan society to deal with serious issues both theological and pastoral. The encounter with Greeks trained in philosophical thought required the Church to express its teaching in philosophical terms. Theological matters dominated the agenda of the ecumenical councils and the treatises of the great fathers—St Athanasius of Alexandria, St Basil of Caesarea, St Gregory of Nazianzus, St Gregory of Nyssa. The practical problems arising for Christian life in a pagan society were the primary concern of St John Chrysostom. Among the recurrent themes of his preaching were the proper use of wealth,[1] the correct attitude to popular entertainments, and the requirements of family life.[2]

St John was raised at Antioch by his widowed mother,

---

[1] See St John Chrysostom, *On Wealth and Poverty,* translation and introduction by Catharine P. Roth (Crestwood: St Vladimir's Seminary Press, 1984).

[2] See M. L. W. Laistner, *Christianity and Pagan Culture in the Later Roman Empire,* together with an English translation of John Chrysostom's "Address on Vainglory and the Right Way for Parents to Bring Up Their Children" (Ithaca: Cornell University Press, 1951; Cornell Paperbacks 1967).

Anthusa. After an education in the pagan classics, he turned
to the study of the Bible, and then to monastic life. After
six years as a monk living in the hills, he was forced by
ill-health to return to the city. He served as reader, deacon,
and priest during twenty years at Antioch. In 398 he was
taken to Constantinople and consecrated bishop. His episcopate in the imperial capital was troubled by controversies
and intrigues, which led to his exile in 404 and death in
407.

St John's earliest writings emphasize the value of celibate life. He wrote to advise his friend Theodore (later
bishop of Mopsuestia) not to abandon the monastic life.[3]
Other works of St John combat the attackers of monasticism[4] and defend the preference for virginity.[5] His early
life as the son of a widow and as a young monk perhaps
failed to give him the opportunity of fully appreciating the
potential for grace in married life. Later, his experience as
a pastor at Antioch and at Constantinople corrected this
imbalance in his understanding, and later he became the
great apologist for Christian marriage. Among his most
faithful friends and helpers was the widow and deaconess
Olympias, who may have taught him through her example
and her conversation (which was continued in their letters[6])
what the quality of a Christian woman could be.

Among the problems for the Church in a still largely
pagan society was the development of a Christian doctrine
of marriage and a Christian form of wedding. The doctrine
of marriage was, of course, based on the Jewish law. Christ
had modified this by forbidding divorce except in the most
extreme case.[7] The Pauline epistles to the Corinthians and

---

[3]PG 47.277-316; English translation in LNPF 9 (1889) 87-116.
[4]PG 47.319-386.
[5]PG 48.533-596.
[6]PG 52.549-623; partial English translation in LNPF 9 (1889)
287-303.
[7]Mt 5.31-32.

Ephesians became the basis for the Christian teaching on marriage and virginity. The celibate life was valued, as it had not been in mainstream Judaism, in view of the imminent approach of the last times.[8] Even when the end of time failed to arrive, the ascetic life in the form of monasticism was recognized as a sign of God's kingdom. At the same time, marriage was accepted as good. God had created humanity as male and female, with the intent that they should join together, even before the fall[9] (though some of the Fathers have taught that sexual procreation was instituted after the fall). Christ blessed the wedding at Cana with His presence and performed a miracle which assisted the joyous celebration of the event.[10] St Paul instructs married people to remain married.[11] St Peter himself was married, and some of Paul's missionary associates seem to have been married couples (Priscilla and Aquila, Andronicus and Junia, Philologus and Julia).[12] Paul elsewhere mentions wives travelling with missionaries.[13] Some writers, especially those in the tradition of St Augustine of Hippo, have spread the opinion that sexual relations are evil in themselves but tolerated within marriage for the purpose of procreation. This is not the general Orthodox view. The consensus of Orthodox teaching is that "the marriage bed is undefiled."[14] The First Council of Nicea (325), at the urging of the ascetic St Paphnutius, upheld the ordination of married men. The Council of Gangra (ca. 340) condemned those who abhor conjugal relations. As Paul Evdokimov says, "Under the grace of the sacrament the sexual life is lived without causing the slightest decline

[8]I Cor 7:25-35.
[9]Gen 1:27-28; 2:24.
[10]John 2:1-11.
[11]I Cor 7:27.
[12]Rom 16:3, 7, 15.
[13]I Cor 9:5.
[14]Heb 13:4.

of the inner life."[15] Marriage, like monasticism, is a sign of God's kingdom, because it begins to restore the unity of mankind (and the cosmos as a whole) which has been broken up by sin. Thus marriage is both a great mystery in itself and represents a greater mystery, the unity of redeemed mankind in Christ.[16]

The Pauline epistles give the impression that in the earliest days of the Church women found a considerable degree of freedom and equality with men, epitomized by St Paul's words, "There is neither Jew nor Greek, there is neither slave nor free, there is neither male nor female; for you are all one in Christ Jesus."[17] The first epistle to the Corinthians, chapter 7, shows an equality between husband and wife in sexual matters. Several women were missionaries or patrons of churches, for example Priscilla, Phoebe, and others mentioned in the conclusion of the epistle to the Romans. As time went on, the roles of women became restricted, probably to avoid provoking too much conflict with the surrounding patriarchal society.[18] If women in a household (wives, daughters, or slaves) became Christians, their husbands, fathers, or masters needed to be assured that the women would remain submissive in other respects. Otherwise life could become very difficult for the women. So in the epistles to the Ephesians and Colossians we find exhortations to all the members of a household to maintain their traditional roles.[19] What was originally a survival strategy for Christian women in pagan households has now become the norm for families where all

---

[15]Paul Evdokimov, *The Sacrament of Love*, translated by Anthony P. Gythiel and Victoria Steadman (Crestwood: St Vladimir's Seminary Press, 1985), p. 17.

[16]Eph 5:32.

[17]Gal 3:28.

[18]See Elizabeth Schüssler Fiorenza, *In Memory of Her* (New York: The Crossroad Publishing Company, 1983), pp. 261-266.

[19]Eph 5:21-6:9; Col 3:18-4:1.

the members are Christians. Henceforth Christian teaching does not aim to overthrow patriarchal domination—indeed it was a long time before Christianity became resolved even to oppose slavery—but rather to mitigate its exercise or at best transform it from within. Between St Paul and the twentieth century, the best in Christian teaching on marriage is represented by St John Chrysostom. While he does not suggest any change in the outward structures of men and women's relationships, he expects them to be transfigured by Christian love. When two become one in Christ, their love can enable them to transcend any limitations imposed by the world. Depending on their spiritual gifts, either one may teach the other, and both together may fill their common life with as much holiness as any monks.

After St John, the theology of married love was largely neglected. In the twentieth century, Russian religious philosophers encountered western secular thought. They realized that Orthodox tradition contained an undeveloped potentiality to address the spiritual meaning of human love. The fruits of their work are available in *Marriage: An Orthodox Perspective,* by Father John Meyendorff,[20] and especially in *The Sacrament of Love,* by Paul Evdokimov.[21] The former sets forth briefly the history of Christian marriage and the teachings of the Orthodox Church on the subject. The latter has many profound things to say about the differences and relationships between men and women in the light of Orthodox tradition.

For a long time there was apparently no specifically Christian wedding ceremony.[22] If a husband and wife

---

[20]Crestwood: St Vladimir's Seminary Press, 1970.

[21]Translated by Anthony P. Gythiel and Victoria Steadman (Crestwood: St Vladimir's Seminary Press, 1985).

[22]See Alvian N. Smirensky, "The Evolution of the Present Rite of Matrimony and Parallel Canonical Developments," *St Vladimir's*

received baptism, their marriage was thereby incorporated
into the body of Christ. If Christians wished to marry,
they were expected to obtain the bishop's permission. As
St Ignatius says, "It is right for men and women who
marry to be united with the consent of the bishop, that
marriage be according to the Lord and not according to
lust."[23] After a marriage had been contracted in accordance
with the civil law, the Church ratified the union as a
Christian marriage by admitting the newlyweds together
to the Holy Communion. It appears from Chrysostom's
sermons that in his time the actual wedding took place in
the home, at a banquet which could be the occasion of unseemly display. He urges that the clergy be invited to
the party in place of the customary pagan singers and
dancers, in order that marriage begin in seriousness and
holiness. Elsewhere Chrysostom refers to wedding crowns.[24]
The rite of crowning seems to have been introduced by the
fourth century as an elaboration of the blessing given to a
newly married couple at the Eucharist. The crowning of
marriages continued to take place at the Eucharist, and to
be culminated by the reception of Holy Communion, as
long as the Roman state maintained a separate system for
registering marriages according to the law. When the state
gave the Church responsibility for all marriages, whether
the men and women involved were committed Christians
or not, it became necessary to provide a wedding ceremony
which could be separated from the Eucharist. So the rite
of crowning began to be used alone. Those couples who
were not able to receive the Holy Communion could instead
share a common cup of wine. This is now the usual form

Seminary Quarterly 8 (1964) 1.38-47; John Meyendorff, *Marriage:
An Orthodox Perspective* (Crestwood: St Vladimir's Seminary
Press, 1970) 18-34.

[23]Ignatius, Letter to Polycarp 5.2.

[24]Homily 9.2 on I Tim.

of wedding in the Orthodox Church. In current practice sometimes the crowning is once again made a part of the Eucharistic Liturgy. In situations of persecution the crowning may be dispensed with, if the couple are less likely to attract dangerous attention by simply receiving Communion.

Along with the development of the wedding ceremony, there followed a development in its interpretation. In the earlier stage, the Church received a natural marriage, made according to human laws, and lifted it up into the kingdom of God. The existing human marriage was transfigured by the Church's blessing. Later on, a more legalistic mentality raised the question, who is the minister of the sacrament of marriage? The western answer was that the couple themselves were the ministers of the sacrament, as they made the contract with each other. The Society of Friends have carried this view to its logical conclusion. The eastern Church, in contrast, decided that the priest must be the minister of the sacrament, as he brought the marriage into being by giving the Church's blessing. In consequence of this difference in the understanding of marriage, the Roman Catholic and Orthodox Churches have different attitudes to divorce. If marriage is essentially a contract undertaken by two parties, it cannot be dissolved except by the death of one of the parties, provided that the right conditions for the contract were met at the beginning. So annulment may be possible but not divorce. If, on the other hand, the sacrament of marriage offers a gift of grace to which human beings may respond inadequately, then the possibility exists that a marriage may fail. But if the couple do respond to the gift of grace, a marriage in the risen Christ should not be dissolved by the death of the body. Hence the Orthodox Church is hardly more willing to approve a marriage after the death of a spouse than after a divorce. Remarriage is forbidden to deacons and priests in either case, as the clergy are expected to teach by their example what the ideal should be for all Christians. When the

Orthodox Church does allow a second marriage, the rite
prescribed differs from the crowning of a first marriage and
has a predominantly penitential character.

The present volume offers the most notable of St John
Chrysostom's writings on marriage. In the course of his
ministry he preached and published a series of sermons on
each of the epistles of St Paul. Naturally the subject of
marriage and family relationships had to arise when he
dealt with the epistles to the Corinthians and Ephesians.
It seems that the homilies on these epistles date from his
years in Antioch.[25] The homilies on the epistle to the
Colossians are attributed to his episcopate in Constantinople.[26] Perhaps also at Constantinople St John wrote a
series of three sermons or treatises on marriage and divorce.
In this volume we present Homily 19 on 1 Corinthians,
Homilies 20 and 21 on Ephesians, and Homily 12 on
Colossians, translated by Father David Anderson, and the
first and third sermons on marriage, translated by Catharine
Roth. These versions are abridged in places. Complete
translations of the homilies on the epistles of St Paul may
be found in the Library of the Fathers of the Holy Catholic
Church.[27] The sermons on marriage have apparently not
previously been published in English, though excerpts
appear in *Women in the Early Church,* by Elizabeth A.
Clark.[28]

St John's Homily 19 on 1 Corinthians 7 deals with the
role of sexual relations in marriage. He emphasizes first of

---

[25]C. Baur, *St John Chrysostom and His Time* (London 1959),
1.298-299.

[26]Baur, 2.93.

[27]Hom 19 on I Cor, LFC 4.245-259; Hom 20-21 on Eph, LFC
6.314-348; Hom 12 on Col, LFC 14.321-334.

[28]*Message of the Fathers of the Church,* general editor Thomas
Halton (Wilmington, Delaware: Michael Glazier, Inc., 1983) vol.
13, pp. 36-37, 63-64.

all the equality of husband and wife in this regard. Neither spouse should seek to abstain from sex without the consent of the other, and even then only temporarily. Such abstinence creates tensions in the home and often leads to adultery and divorce. St John seems to be addressing some women in particular who have thought that they were practicing a righteous asceticism in abstaining from sex. He tells them that the continence which they think virtuous is actually sinful because of the harm it does to their marriage. Indeed, the proper valuation of sexual love is still a problem for Christian couples. Moral theologians have said too much about the value of virginity and about the sinfulness of the flesh, and too little about the possibility of a transfigured human love. Some hagiography gives the impression that married saints are those who gave up their marital relations to live as brother and sister.[29] This is not the way for most of us. As Evdokimov says, "It is not 'in spite of marriage,' but in its fulfillment that spouses live the supernatural and holiness of their union."[30]

Continuing the subject of equality, St John speaks of the Lord's prohibition of divorce. Neither spouse may divorce the other and remarry. St John recommends that even when a separation occurs, the couple ought to remain living in the same house. This may seem unrealistic, but he hopes that a reconciliation may take place. Besides, he is probably considering the wife's welfare. In the social conditions of his time, a divorced woman may have had difficulty in living independently, and may have been forced to seek the protection and support of another husband. The subject of divorce leads to the question of marriage with an unbeliever. St John points out that St Paul

---

[29]See Christos Yannaras, *The Freedom of Morality*, translated by Elizabeth Brière (Crestwood: St Vladimir's Seminary Press, 1984), p. 167 n. 30.

[30]Evdokimov 163.

did not say that a Christian might marry an unbeliever, but
that one might become a Christian while already married
to an unbeliever. In that case one ought to remain married
if the unbelieving spouse is willing to tolerate the Christian's differing religious practices. The Christian partner
must not participate in pagan rituals. St John does not
say how much restriction on Christian practices may be
accepted, although he does recommend discretion in attempts to convert a husband by persuasion. In this case
of mixed marriages, St John again reassures those women
who are worried that it may be wrong to have marital
relations with an unbeliever. The pure faith of a believing
wife can sanctify the marriage and the children which may
be born from it. Besides, the wife may convert her husband if she approaches him in the right way. St Paul's
advice to remain in the state in which you were called
then leads from married people to slaves and to unmarried
people. Interpreting an obscure text, St John urges slaves
to seek freedom from evil rather than freedom from their
masters. In advising unmarried people to remain single,
St John emphasizes the requirement that a virgin should
really be devoting herself to the Lord and not merely
avoiding involvement with a husband. It is not sex which
is evil, but excessive attachment to the affairs of the world.
Whether single or married, we can all pursue holiness and
seek the kingdom of heaven.

When St John comes to expound the epistle to the
Ephesians, he must discuss the famous passage of chapter
5 in which St Paul compares the relationship of husband
and wife with that of Christ and the Church. Modern
scholars contrast the seeming inequality here with the
equality expressed in 1 Corinthians. For this and other
reasons, they say that this epistle was written by a follower
of St Paul, not Paul himself. St John does not suggest any
doubts about the authorship. He assumes that the two
texts can be reconciled. Here, he is concerned to set forth

the responsibilities of both partners in a marriage. Both must strive to maintain harmony, to recreate the unity which God established at the beginning when He created them male and female and directed them to be one flesh. Incidentally, St John seems to have changed the views which he expressed in his early treatise "On Virginity." There he said that God did not create man for marriage before the fall, whereas here he emphasizes the unity of Adam and Eve. Within the nuptial unity, he goes on to say, husband and wife have different roles. The wife must obey her husband, considering her obedience a part of her duty to the Lord even if she is not inclined to obedience for her husband's sake. The husband, as he hopes to receive obedience, must treat his wife with loving care. Then she will respond willingly as a free person and not fearfully like a slave. He must persist in loving her whatever her faults may be and whatever the consequences may be, as Christ loved the Church and died for her even before He had purified her. The wife's duty is to respect her husband, but the husband's duty is greater, as love is a stronger force than fear. We are not excused from our duties by our spouse's delinquency. A wife must still respect an unloving husband; a husband must still love a disrespectful wife. There are limits, however. As St John says in Homily 19 on 1 Corinthians, a wife should not obey if her husband asks her to do something wrong. It is not entirely clear what a husband should do with an unfaithful wife. He is permitted to divorce her, but the trend of what St John says would suggest that forgiving her might be better.

When St Paul says that marriage is a great mystery, St John insists that we must not pass over the primary meaning. Human marriage is a great mystery, because two join together and become one. It is also a sign of the greater mystery, that Christ became one with the Church. St John points out that St Paul would not have used marriage as an analogy for Christ and the Church if physical

unity were not something good. The unity of husband and
wife extends to their children and servants. The man who
properly oversees his whole household can make it a little
church which will promote the spiritual growth of all its
members.

From this more theoretical discussion, St John turns
to some specific advice on ways to preserve marital harmony. Most of this advice is as applicable now as ever.
Husbands and wives should trust each other and not believe
unsubstantiated accusations made by a third party. A husband should not mind if his wife demands more of his time,
because this shows her love for him. A wife should not nag
her husband for not making enough money, but should
value his company. A husband should use gentle words and
his example to teach his wife to be virtuous—not to desire
high social position, expensive clothes and jewelry, or
extravagant furnishings in the house. Elsewhere St John
gives some advice which complements this, suggesting how
a wife may teach her husband virtue by her example.[31] A
husband should always begin his admonitions by telling his
wife how much he loves her. He should enjoy being at
home with her. He should praise her in front of others but
advise her privately and patiently. They should pray together at home, attend church together, and again at
home discuss together the readings which they have heard
in church. If they give dinner parties, they should invite
not only their friends but also the poor. For St John, alms-
giving is one of the greatest Christian duties for those who
have the means. A husband and wife should consider both
their bodies and all their possessions common property.
Neither one should speak of "mine" and "yours." If they
must endure poverty, they should accept it with courage
and trust in God. Married people who live like this can
become as holy as any monks. They can guide their chil-

---

[31]Hom 61 on the Gospel of John.

dren (and their servants) in such a way that the whole household may join them in acquiring holiness.

The relationship of children and parents is discussed further in the following homily, which expounds the next passage of the epistle to the Ephesians (6:1-4). Children and parents each have certain duties towards the other. Children should obey their parents. Beginning with the honor which they owe to their parents, they should learn how to treat other people with the proper respect and kindness. As in the case of wives, the duty of obedience is qualified. St Paul says, "Obey your parents in the Lord."[32] If your parents ask you to do something wrong, St John says, that is not "in the Lord," and you should not obey. From the duties of children he turns to discuss the duties of parents, a subject which he treats in more detail in his "Address on Vainglory and the Right Way for Parents to Bring Up Their Children."[33] If parents expect their children to be obedient, they must train the children in virtue. Above all, they should read the Bible together, to provide good examples which may counteract the bad examples offered by worldly entertainments. Now that the worldly entertainments come right into our homes by television, it is surely even more important to read the Bible and other edifying stories with our children. While not denying the value of education, St John thinks it more necessary to raise children with a true sense of values than to teach them a lucrative trade or profession. If we teach them virtue, we reveal the image of God which is within them. We are responsible to God not only for our own righteousness, but for our wives' and children's characters as well. Wives may also have some responsibility for their husbands, as they certainly have for their chil-

---

[32]Eph 6:1.
[33]Laistner, Appendix 93-122.

dren.[34] If we do our best to educate ourselves and our
families in virtue, then God will assist us to bring the
work to perfection.

"Remember my bonds," St Paul says in concluding the
epistle to the Colossians (4:18). This phrase is enough to
start St John speaking about the bonds of marriage. Evi-
dently he was impelled more this time by the needs of his
congregation than by the requirements of the text. He de-
plores the wedding customs of his society, perhaps in
particular of the wealthy court circles in Constantinople.
He expresses most vehemently his conviction that marriage
is holy and that people are failing to show it due respect.
Obviously the Christians (those who could afford it, any-
way) had carried over the pagan practice of holding wedding parties with lewd dancing and singing. In origin all
this would have been a fertility ritual, but it was out of
place in the celebration of a Christian marriage. St John
insists that marriage is a great mystery. "Mystery" not only
means something strange and marvelous but is also the
word used for the sacraments of the Church. St John speaks
in very positive terms about the pleasure of the sexual act
by which husband and wife become one. He thinks of the
child as a kind of bridge which joins the flesh of the mother
and father. Then, to keep the metaphor from going too far,
he adds that the husband and wife are still one flesh even
if there is no child. St John is very far from the Augustinian
view in which sexual pleasure is basically sinful but tolerated
only for the sake of procreation. Here the union of husband
and wife is recognized as good in its own right.

If marriage is good, then it ought to be celebrated in a
holy manner. Before anything else, you should choose a
virtuous husband for your daughter. This advice provides
a counterpart to his sermon on "How to Choose a Wife"
(see below). When you celebrate the wedding, you may

---

[34]Hom 9 on I Tim; Hom 61 on John.

hold a dinner party, but you should not spend a lot of money on decorations, clothing, and entertainers. You should not borrow things which may get broken or lost and give you extra worries. If there are songs, they should be edifying songs. There should be spiritual joy instead of drunkenness. You should invite Christ to be present at the wedding by inviting the poor and the clergy. In St John's time, apparently, the wedding was held in the home, though the Church's blessing was given at the Eucharist, when the newly married couple received Communion together and perhaps were crowned. Although wedding customs may differ now, there is still room for a warning against excessive spending, ostentatious display, and riotous partying. There is still need to enter a Christian marriage with a sober respect for the dignity of the sacrament, so that the whole married life may be a progress together toward holiness.

In the first of St John's three sermons on marriage, he takes as his text 1 Corinthians 7:1-4. His main theme is that marriage is intended to promote virtue. St Paul expresses this negatively in saying that people should marry "because of the temptation to immorality" (literally, "because of fornication"). First St John points out that if marriage is the good remedy which eliminates immorality, our wedding customs ought to help us obtain God's blessing. St John criticizes the weddings of his time, as he did in Homily 12 on Colossians. Here he especially emphasizes the value of inviting the poor to your wedding banquet. If you feed the poor, their prayers will help you to obtain healthy children and a long, happy life. Next, St John discusses the reasons for the institution of marriage. There are two, he says: for the procreation of children and for the chastity of the couple themselves. Now that the earth is filled with people, he says, there is no great need for procreation. Besides, since Christ has given us the hope of resurrection, we do not need children to perpetuate us.

Therefore, St John says, the more important reason for marriage is to give us chastity. The virtue of chastity must be understood positively. It is not merely avoidance of immorality, but integrity of the person, body and soul, and direction of oneself towards holiness. This is possible as much for the two who are made one in marriage as for the celibate person. So the primary reason for marriage is the unity in love and holiness of the couple themselves, not the good of society or the reproduction of the species. Evdokimov calls this the "personalistic conception of marriage."[35] Finally, St John speaks of the equal responsibility of husband and wife to preserve nuptial chastity. The "double standard" prevailing in society and Roman law is not acceptable for Christians. Husbands must be just as faithful as they expect their wives to be. In the second sermon of this series (not included in this volume), St John deals with divorce and remarriage.

In the third sermon, St John addresses men who want to marry and gives them advice on how to choose a wife. He gave similar advice on the choice of husbands in his Homily 12 on Colossians. Here he begins by insisting on the importance of the subject. As divorce is forbidden to Christians, except in the case of adultery, a man will have to put up with his wife no matter how she turns out. So he should be careful about his choice in the first place. As in his Homily 20 on Ephesians, St John reminds the prospective husband how much Christ endured and continues to endure for the Church with all her faults. A husband must be patient with his wife especially because they have the same origin, namely that Eve was made from Adam's side. St John again stresses the basic meaning of "This is a great mystery." Marriage itself is a mystery, in that the parents happily give up their children and the newlyweds leave everyone else to join with each other. The mystery

---

[35]Evdokimov 41-45.

of marriage is not diminished by the fact that it also symbolizes the union of Christ and the Church.

St John goes on to speak in more detail of what a man may expect from his wife. He should not hope to get rich by "marrying money," any more than a woman should.[36] He may, however, expect his wife to manage his household, to take charge of the servants and organize all the domestic work. St John does not believe that women have the ability to manage outside businesses or public affairs. Probably he would have said that the charitable activities of the deaconess Olympias, which must have required considerable managerial capability, were simply household management on a larger scale. The bishop is not, however, entirely satisfied with the social role of upper-class women in his time. This shows in his paradigmatic narrative of Isaac and Rebecca's marriage. Rebecca did not stay at home, enclosed in the women's quarters, letting servants do all the work for her. She went out every day to carry water and encountered strangers without harm to her virtue. She was physically fit enough to leap off a camel, yet modest enough to veil herself when Isaac came in sight. Even in Constantinople there must have been many less affluent young women who did their own shopping and carried their own burdens, though St John does not mention them. Perhaps under different circumstances he would have accepted that work could be distributed in different ways between men and women. In any case, each husband and wife must find some way to make their roles complementary and to avoid rivalry. They will surely agree with St John's goal for marriage, that it should provide a haven of comfort and happiness amid the storms of life. A marriage should begin with God's blessing, proceed in harmony and vitrtuous living, and finally lead the whole family to the kingdom of heaven.

---

[36]Hom 12 on Col.

I wish to express my gratitude for their assistance and encouragement to Bishop Kallistos of Diocleia, Presbytera Sophronia Tomaras, and especially to Father Gregory Roth, Nathaniel, and Margaret, who have taught me what little I know about marriage and family life.

                              —Catharine P. Roth
                              Oakwood, Ohio
                              December 1985

HOMILY 19
On 1 Corinthians 7

*Now concerning the matters about which you wrote.
It is well for a man not to touch a woman. But
because of the temptation to immorality, each man
should have his own wife and each woman her own
husband. (v. 1-2)*

In previous chapters of this epistle, St Paul corrects
the three most unpleasant problems of the Corinthian
church: first, factionalism within the Chuch; second, the
man living in incest; and third, the greed which was causing
members of the Church to sue each other in the public
courts. Here, however, he speaks more gently. He gives
his audience a rest from such vulgarities and inserts some
advice and exhortation concerning marriage and virginity.
Notice that in 2 Corinthians he does the opposite: he begins with lighter issues, and ends with more serious ones.
But in this epistle, after he finishes his discourse on virginity, he returns again to more alarming subjects. He does
not follow an exact order, but varies his words, sometimes
speaking sternly and sometimes gently, as the occasion
requires.

He says, "Now concerning the matters about which you
wrote." They had written to ask if it was right for a man
to abstain from relations with his wife. He answers their
questions and establishes rules for married life, but places
his reply within the context of virginity: "It is well for a

man not to touch a woman." It is as if he were saying, "If you are searching for the best and most lofty path, then do not take a woman at all. But if you want help and security in your weakness, look for a wife." Within marriage, both then and now, one of two things is likely to happen: either the husband wants to have relations with his wife, but she does not, or vice versa. Notice that he speaks of both situations in the same way. Some have claimed, incidentally, that St Paul was asked this question in reference to the clergy. But I cannot agree with this, because his advice is not given to a particular group of people, but to everyone in general. If he were writing only for priests, he would have said, "It is well for a *teacher* not to touch a woman." But he speaks generally: "It is well for a *man* . . .," he says, not only for a priest. Later on he says, "Are you free from a wife? Do not seek marriage." He does not mention priests or teachers, but speaks indefinitely, and continues in this tone for the rest of the passage. By saying, "But because of the temptation to immorality, each man should have his own wife," he uses this solution to temptation to guide men to the practice of self control.

"The husband should give to his wife her conjugal rights,[1] and likewise the wife to her husband" (v. 3). And what are conjugal rights? First, it means that the wife has no power over her own body, but she is her husband's slave—and also his ruler. If you refuse to serve your husband properly, you offend God. So, wife, if you want to abstain, even for a little while, get your husband's permission first. That is why St Paul speaks of conjugal rights as a *debt*; to show that neither husband nor wife is his or her own master, but rather are each other's servants. As

---

[1] So the RSV. St John Chrysostom's Greek text of the Scriptures used τὴν ὀφειλομένην εὔνοιαν which literally means, "Let the husband pay his debt of honor to his wife."

for you, husband, if a prostitute tries to seduce you, tell her, "My body is not my own, but my wife's." And let the wife say the same to any man attempting to undermine her fidelity: "My body is not my own, but my husband's." So if neither husband nor wife has power over their own bodies, they have even less control over money. Listen carefully, all married men and women: if you cannot call your body your own, then you certainly cannot call your money your own. Now I admit that elsewhere in Scripture, both in the Old and New Testaments, men are given far greater authority: "Your desire shall be for your husband, and he shall rule over you,"[2] or, "Husbands, love your wives . . . and let the wife see that she respects her husband;"[3] notice Paul's choice of words. In this passage, however, there is no mention of greater or lesser authority. Why does he speak here in terms of equality? Because his subject is conjugal fidelity. He intends for the husband to have the greater responsibility in nearly every concern, but fidelity is an exception: "The husband does not rule over his own body, but the wife does." Husband and wife are equally responsible for the honor of their marriage bed.

"Do not refuse[4] one another except by agreement" (v. 5). What does this really mean? Paul is saying that the wife should not abstain without the husband's consent, and vice versa. Why? Because great evils—adulteries, fornications and broken homes among them—have often resulted from this kind of abstinence. If men fornicate even when they have the consolation of their wives, what do you expect will happen if they are deprived of this? No wonder Paul calls such a refusal an act of fraud, just as he has spoken

---

[2]Gen 3:16.

[3]Eph 5:25, 33.

[4]"Refuse" is a very weak translation of ἀποστερεῖτε. Older translations (Vulgate, KJV) use "defraud" which is certainly the way Chrysostom interprets the phrase.

of conjugal rights as a debt to be paid, in order to show
the importance of mutual authority within marriage. If one
abstains without the other's consent, it is an act of fraud;
but if consent is given, it is not, just as if you took something of mine that I had already given you, I could not
call it theft. Theft occurs only if you take something by
force, without my consent. This is what many wives do
when they refuse their husbands. They commit a sin which
outweighs the righteousness of their abstinence. They are
responsible for their husband's licentiousness and the
broken homes that result. Instead of behaving this way,
they should value harmony above everything; nothing is
more important. Let us examine these things more closely:
imagine a household in which the wife abstains from
marital relations without her husband's consent. Suppose
he commits fornication, or on the other hand remains
continent but frets and complains, loses his temper, and
constantly fights with his wife. Either way, what good is
all the fasting and continence? No good at all; it has
broken love to pieces. How much abuse, trouble, and fight-
ing has resulted from this!

When husband and wife are at odds with one another,
their household is in no better shape than a storm-tossed
ship in which the captain and the pilot disagree. That is
why Paul says: "Do not refuse one another except by agreement for a season, that you may devote yourselves to
prayer." He is referring to unusually intense prayer. Otherwise, if he forbids those who have marital relations to
pray, his words about ceaseless prayer would have no
meaning. It is certainly possible to be married and to pray
at the same time, but prayer can be intensified by abstinence. Notice that he does not merely say, ". . . that you may
pray," but, ". . . that you may *devote* yourselves to prayer."
He does not mean that sexual relations would make the
prayer unclean. He simply means that they occupy one's
attention. "But then come together again, lest Satan tempt

you." In order that he may not seem to be legislating arbitrarily, he offers an explanation: "Lest Satan tempt you . . ." And to demonstrate that the devil is not solely responsible for temptations to adultery, he says, "Lest Satan tempt you *through lack of self-control*." "I say this by way of concession, not of command. I wish that all were as I myself am" (in a state of continence). He often uses himself as an example when speaking of difficult matters: "Be imitators of me."[5]

"But each has his own special gift from God, one of one kind and one of another" (v. 7). He says this to encourage the Corinthians, since he has just sternly accused them of lacking self-control. "Each has his own special gift from God;" he doesn't mean that we don't have to strive zealously for self-control, but simply wants to comfort them, as I have just said. If self-control is a gift, and man can't attain it by his efforts, how could he say, "To the unmarried and the widows I say that it is well for them to remain single as I do. But if they cannot exercise self-control, they should marry" (v. 8-9). You can see Paul's common sense here. He says that continence is better, but does not force a person who cannot attain it, fearing that defeat may result. "For it is better to marry than to be aflame with passion" (v. 9); here he shows how great a tyranny the passions exercise over us. What he means is something like this: if you suffer with violent, burning passion, then relieve your pain and sweat through marriage, before you utterly collapse.

"To the married I give charge, not I but the Lord . . ." (v. 10). He says "not I" here because he is about to quote a law which Christ Himself established, that a man cannot divorce his wife except for reasons of unchastity. Paul's previous words, though not explicitly spoken by Christ, was nevertheless inspired by Him. There, however, Christ

---

[5]1 Cor 4:16.

speaks specifically. That is the difference between "I" and "not I." Never imagine Paul's words to be merely human opinion, since he says, "I think that I have the Spirit of God" (v. 40). Now what exactly does the Lord command married couples? "The wife should not separate from her husband, but if she does, let her remain single or else be reconciled to her husband, and that the husband should not divorce his wife" (v. 10-11). Since we see that separations occur, whether caused by abstinence, pettiness, or other motives, he says that although it would be better for such things never to happen, when they do happen, the wife should still remain with her husband. Even if they don't have sexual relations, at least she won't take another man to be her husband.

"To the rest I say, not the Lord, that if any brother has a wife who is an unbeliever, and she consents to live with him, he should not divorce her. If any woman has a husband who is an unbeliever, and he consents to live with her, she should not divorce him" (v. 12-13). Earlier in this epistle,[6] when Paul warns us not to associate with immoral men, he corrects himself by restricting his prohibition to immoral men[7] *among the brethren.* He does this to make things easier; otherwise we would have to leave this world. So also here, he provides us with the easiest solution: "If a wife has an unbelieving husband, or vice versa, let not one leave the other." What do you think of that? Does it surprise you that, although unbelief is worse than fornication, an unbeliever is to remain with his spouse, but fornication is grounds for separation? Fornication is indeed the lesser sin, but here God in His great mercy shows us that the lesser sins can prevent us from conquering the greater. For instance, Christ says in the Gospel: "Leave your gift here before the altar and go; *first* be reconciled to your

---

[6]Cf 1 Cor 5:9-11.
[7]Literally, *fornicators.*

brother, and then come and offer your gift."[8] Consider
also the man who owed ten thousand talents.[9] God didn't
punish him because he couldn't pay the money, but because
he refused to forgive a fellow-servant who owed him a
hundred denarii. (Likewise, fornication might be a lesser
evil, but where it remains secure, unbelief will never be
overthrown. St Paul also realized that a Christian wife
might worry that intercourse with an unbelieving husband
is an impure act. He dispels such fears by saying, "The
unbelieving husband is sanctified[10] through his wife, and
the unbelieving wife is sanctified through her husband"
(v. 14). Yet earlier he said, "Do you not know that he
who joins himself to a prostitute becomes one body with
her?"[11] We might then conclude that a woman joined to
an unbelieving idolter becomes one body with him. Is
there a contradiction here? No, because although they
become one body, the woman is not defiled, since the
purity of her faith is stronger than the impurity of his
unbelief. Likewise the purity of a believing husband is
stronger than the impurity of an unbelieving wife.

How can it be that a husband would not be criticized
for throwing a wife who had become a prostitute out of his
house, but in the case of an unbelieving spouse, impurity is
overcome and sexual relations are permitted? Because there
is hope that the spouse who is perishing through his unbelief might be saved through marriage to a believer. In the
former situation, however, the marriage has already been
dissolved: both partners are tainted, while here only one
is really to blame. This is what I mean: an unfaithful wife
has defiled the sexual act itself. If her husband has
intercourse with her, he becomes as impure as she is, since

---

[8]Mt 5:24.
[9]Cf Mt 18:23ff.
[10]RSV *consecrated.*
[11]1 Cor 6:16.

both of them become one body. Purity in such a situation is impossible for husband or wife, but here it is not the case. How is this possible? An unbelieving husband is impure because of his unbelief; but if his believing wife is not united to him *in the act of unbelief,* she remains pure. He remains impure as far as his unbelief is concerned; but since marriage means physical union, the sexual act through which he and his wife are joined is not affected by his unbelief. Also, there is hope that this man will be converted by his wife's influence, but in the other situation it wouldn't be very easy. Once an unfaithful wife has dishonored and wronged her husband by becoming another man's, and ignoring the duties of marriage, how can she win him back, especially if they remain as strangers to each other? A husband is no longer a husband after such infidelity, but in the other case, even if a wife is not a believer, it does not destroy the husband's marriage rights. Bear in mind, however, that he is not recommending indiscriminate marriages with unbelievers. That is why he says, ". . . and he (the unbelieving partner) *consents* to live with her (the believer)."

Tell me, then, what harm is there in such a marriage? The purity of the faith is upheld, and there is plenty of hope for the unbelieving partner. Such marriages should be left in peace. There is no reason to introduce unnecessary tension. But remember: the issue here does not concern those who are contemplating marriage, but only those who are already married. He did not say, "If any brother wants to marry an unbeliever," but, "If any brother *has* a wife who is an unbeliever." This means that if anyone receives the Word of Truth *after* getting married, and the wife remains an unbeliever but wants the marriage to continue, then it should not be broken. "For the unbelieving husband is sanctified through his wife." The purity of the believer is the stronger force. But how can an unbeliever be holy? It is impossible, but notice that Paul does not say that he *is* holy, but that he is sanctified *through* his wife. And this does not mean that his unbelief becomes holy, but that the strong word "holy" is intended to dispel his wife's fear as completely as possible, and to lead him to desire the truth. Impurity does not originate in the union of their bodies, but in their thoughts and motives. Here is the proof: if one partner remains unclean when a child is begotten, then the child would have to be either unclean or only half clean, but Paul says the child is clean: "Otherwise your children would be unclean, but as it is they are *holy*" (v. 14). Again, he uses the explicit word "holy" instead of "not unclean" to cast out the fears that arise from suspicions of this kind.

"But if the unbelieving partner separates himself, let it be so" (v. 15). How does he "separate himself"? Here conjugal infidelity is not the question, but what if he tries to force you to sacrifice to idols, or to join with him in some immoral act, on the grounds of marriage, and when you refuse, he leaves you? Well, let him go; it is better to break up the marriage for righteousness' sake. Paul elaborates: "In such a case the brother or sister is not bound." If he beats you every day, constantly picking fights over this issue, it is better to separate. These are the conditions Paul visualizes when he says, "For God has called you to peace." The unbelieving partner is as much to blame for such a separation as the partner guilty of infidelity.

"Wife, how do you know whether you will save your husband?" (v. 16). He is elaborating here on his admonition that "she should not divorce him." It is as if Paul were saying, "If your husband is not contentious, it could very well prove to be worthwhile if you stay with him. So stay, give him advice, persuade him of the truth." No teacher is so effective as a persuasive wife. Notice, however, that St Paul doesn't forcibly impose this idea, and demand that every spouse, no matter what the circumstances, attempt to persuade his partner in this way; such a demand would be too burdensome. On the other hand, he doesn't recommend the whole situation to be dismissed as hopeless. He realizes that much is uncertain, so he leaves things in the air: "Wife, how do you know whether you will save your husband? Husband, how do you know whether you will save your wife? Only, let every one lead the life which the Lord has assigned to him, and in which God has called him. Was anyone at the time of his call already circumcised? Let him not seek to remove the marks of circumcision. Was anyone at the time of his call uncircumcised? Let him not seek circumcision. For neither circumcision counts for anything, nor uncircumcision, but keeping the commandments of God. Everyone should remain in the state in which he was called. Were you a slave when called? Never mind" (vs. 17-21). None of these things contributes anything to the faith, so don't argue about them or be confused by them, since the faith has overthrown all these things. "Everyone should remain in the state in which he was called." Was your wife an unbeliever when you were called? Stay together; don't send her away because you think the faith demands it. Were you a slave when called? It doesn't matter; continue on as a slave. Had you not been circumcised when you were called? Stay uncircumcised. Were you already circumcised, when you became a believer? Don't try to remove the marks of your circumcision. That is what "let everyone lead the life which the Lord has assigned to Him" means. None of these circumstances hinder a godly life. Whether you are a slave, or have an unbelieving wife, or are marked with the sign of circumcision, you are called to faith, and that is what matters.

Amazing! Look what he says about slavery! Just as circumcision is no advantage towards salvation, and uncircumcision no hindrance, so also slavery or freedom do not matter either. In order to make this assertion perfectly clear, he says, "But if you can gain your freedom, make use of your present condition instead" (v. 21).[12] For what possible reason should a slave who could be set free choose to remain a slave? Paul is saying that slavery does no harm, but is actually an advantage! I am aware that some people interpret these words to mean, "But if you can gain your freedom, avail yourself of the opportunity." This interpretation, however, does not coincide with Paul's purpose. He is trying to comfort slaves, and to reassure them that their condition does not hinder their salvation. Why would he suddenly urge them to seek freedom? On the contrary, he realizes that someone would ask, "What can I possibly do? I cannot obtain freedom, but as a slave I am wronged and degraded continually." So he certainly is not urging them to seek freedom, but intends to show that a slave gains nothing by being set free, saying, "Even if you have it in your power to be set free, remain a slave." But he adds this explanation: "For he who was called in the Lord as a slave is a freedman of the Lord. Likewise he who was free when called is a slave of Christ" (v. 22). As far as Christ is concerned, both slave and master are equal. Are you the slave of Christ? So is your master! In what way is the slave a freedman? Because Christ has freed you not only from sin, but also from slavery to external evils. Even though you remain a slave, as far as earthly life is concerned, in Christ's eyes you are not a slave. This is a great wonder; how can a slave be simultaneously enslaved and free? If he is freed from the passions, and from

---

[12]The meaning of μᾶλλον χρῆσαι is impossible to determine from the Scriptural text itself. The KJV and Douay-Rheims translate this phrase literally, and therefore do not answer the question. Among modern translations, the RSV conjectures that such a slave should avail himself of the opportunity for freedom, while providing in a footnote the alternative translation, that he should remain a slave making use of his present condition (Chrysostom's exegesis). The NEB and *Today's English Version* do the same.

vices of the mind; if he disdains riches, and refrains from
anger and all the other passions, then he is truly free.

"You were bought with a price; do not become slaves
of men" (v. 23). These words are addressed not only to
slaves, but to free men as well. One can be a slave, yet
be free, just as one can be free, but in fact a slave. Again,
how can a slave be simultaneously enslaved and free?
When he does everything for God's sake, deceives no one,
and doesn't shirk the work assigned to him: that is how
someone held in bondage to another can be free. And how
can a free man become a slave? When he serves other men
whose goals are evil, whether they are gluttony, or the lust
for riches, or political power. Such a person, even though
he is free, is more a slave than any man. Consider the
examples of Joseph and his master's wife:[13] Joseph was a
slave, but not a slave to men, so that even in slavery he
was more free than all free men. He didn't yield to the
woman; he wouldn't submit to her wishes. On the other
hand, she was free, but no woman ever acted more like a
slave, begging and fawning over her own servant. But she
didn't succeed. Joseph was free, and he wouldn't do what
she wanted. This is not slavery, but freedom of the highest
kind. Did Joseph's condition of slavery prevent him from
practicing virtue in any way? Pay attention to me, both
free men and slaves: which of these two was really the
slave? Joseph, who resisted temptation and ignored her
advances, or his master's wife, who tried to seduce him?
God has set limits to the obedience a slave owes his master.
He has commanded when one should obey and when one
should not. When your master doesn't order you to do
something displeasing to God, it is right to obey him,
but your obligation goes no further. That is how a slave is
really free. But if you transgress God's law, you become a
slave even if you appear to be free. This is what Paul

---

[13]Cf Gen 39:6 ff.

means when he says, "Do not become slaves of men."
What else could he mean? If he is urging slaves to abandon
their masters and fight for freedom why does he say,
"In whatever state each was called, there let him remain with God" (v. 24)? In another place he says, "Let
all who are under the yoke of slavery regard their masters
as worthy of all honor . . . Those who have believing
masters must not be disrespectful on the ground that they
are brethren; rather they must serve all the better since
those who benefit by their service are believers and beloved."[14] In the epistles to the Ephesians and the Colossians
he commands the same. So it is obvious that Paul's inten-
tion is not to abolish slavery as a social institution. Rather,
he attacks slavery in its worst form, the slavery to evil,
which pays no respect to any external freedom. Joseph's
brothers all had their freedom while he was a slave in
Egypt, but what good did it do them? Were they not in
greater bondage than any slave? They lied to their father.
They sold their brother to the traders under false pretences.
But Joseph was truly free everywhere and in every situation. Freedom is most radiant when it shines through bondage.

Such is the nature of Christianity: even in slavery it
bestows freedom. If someone claimed to have an immortal
body, he would have to prove his claim by being shot
with an arrow and suffering no harm. Likewise, a man
shows he is truly free when his spirit remains unfettered
even though he is subject to masters. That is why St Paul
advises such a person to remain a slave. And if it is impossible for a slave to be a good Christian, then the
pagans will conclude that our religion is very weak; but if
we can convince them that slavery is no impediment to
holiness, they will be amazed at our doctrine. We are not
harmed by chains, or flogging, or death itself; how then

---

[14] 1 Tim 6:1-2.

can slavery hurt us? The faithful have endured fire, sword,
innumerable tortures, anguish, poverty, wild beasts, and
countless sufferings even worse than these without injury—
yes, they have even been strengthened by them. How can
slavery hurt them? It is not slavery that injures us, beloved;
the real slavery is slavery to sin. If you are not held in
bondage to sin, rejoice and have no fear; no one can harm
you, since you are made of such stuff that no one can en-
slave. But if you are a slave of sin, I tell you that even
if you are free ten thousand times over, it is of no advantage to you. Can you tell me what advantage a man has
who, although not in bondage to another man, is in con-
stant subjection to his own passions? At least men are
merciful from time to time, but the passions—they won't
be satisfied until they have destroyed you! Are you another
man's slave? Well, your master is also enslaved to you:
he has to provide you with food, take care of your health,
and provide you with clothing, shoes, and every other
need. You have to take care not to offend your master,
but his cares for your material welfare are greater. Does
he recline at table, while you stand and serve him? So
what! The reverse also is true. Often while you are lying
in bed sleeping sweetly, your master is not only standing,
but keeping a most unpleasant vigil in a marketplace full
of strife.

Tell me, who suffered more? Joseph, or his master's
wife, enslaved to her evil desire? He wouldn't do what
she wanted, but she was very obedient to the licentious
mistress within her, who would not let her alone until she
had completely dishonored herself. What human master,
what savage tyrant could make such a command? "Beg
your slave," it hissed, "flatter this captive bought with
your own silver. Even if he spurns you, continue to pursue him. If you nag him and he still won't consent, wait
until he's alone and try to force him. Act as ridiculously as
possible." How could anything be more dishonorable or

shameful? "And if none of this works, accuse him falsely and deceive your husband." Notice how shamefully servile these commands are, how cruel, harsh, and frenzied. What slave was ever governed by his master as that royal woman was ruled by her lust? She had even lost the ability to disobey. Joseph, on the other hand, was nothing like this. Everything he did brought him glory and honor.

I will tell you about another man enslaved to an even worse mistress, whose commands he dared not disobey. Consider Cain, and his ruler Lady Jealousy. She ordered him to murder his brother Abel, to lie to God, to grieve his father. He shamelessly did all these things, disobeying nothing. Don't be amazed that Jealousy has such great power over one man; she has often destroyed entire nations! For example, the Midianite women used their beauty to deceitfully provoke the Jews to idolatry,[15] and because of this God commanded Israel to destroy their whole nation! This is the kind of slavery Paul is attacking when he says, "Do not become slaves of men." He means, "Don't listen to people who order you to do disgusting things, and don't be enslaved to your own wild impulses."

So, after he has raised their minds to higher things, he continues his message: "Now concerning the virgins[16] I have no command of the Lord, but I give my opinion as one who by the Lord's mercy is trustworthy" (v. 25). The next topic on his agenda is virginity. He has saved it with the hope that they have learned from his previous words to practice continence, and can now advance to greater things. "I have no command," he says, but he knows virginity to be a good thing. Why? For the same reason continence is good: it is well for a person to remain as he is. "Are you bound to a wife? Do not seek to be

---

[15]Cf Num 25.

[16]τῶν παρθένων: RSV translates this as "the unmarried"—certainly quite an assumption!

free. Are you fre from a wife? Do not seek marriage"
(v. 27). He is not contradicting what he said earlier about
abstinence from sexual relations. His advice here is the
same. "Do not refuse one another except by agreement . . .
Are you bound to a wife? Do not seek to be free." There
is no contradiction. Abstinence *without* mutual consent is
forbidden, but if husband and wife *agree* to live together
in continence, they are not seeking to break up their marriage and be free from each other.

This particular advice does not have the force of law.
That is why he says, "But if you marry, you do not sin"
(v. 28). He then speaks of contemporary conditions: the
"present distress," how "the appointed time has grown very
short," and how those who marry will have "affliction."
Marriage entails many things, and he has summarized them
both here, by saying "You are bound," and in his advice
about continence, when he says, "The wife does not
rule over her own body." "But if you marry, you do not
sin." He does not mean someone who has vowed to remain a virgin. She would be sinning if she married, because
if widows incur condemnation for violating their pledge
and seeking second marriage,[17] the judgment for virgins
would be even greater.

"Yet those who marry will have worldly troubles." Ah,
but they will also have pleasure, you say. "But not for
long," Paul replies, for "the time has grown very short"
(v. 29). It is as if he were saying, "We are directed to
leave earthly cares behind us, but you are more deeply
sinking into them." Even if marriage had no troubles, it
would still be better for us to press forward toward the
things yet to come. But since marriage does have its
troubles, why be further burdened by it? Why struggle
under such a weight? Even after you take it you have

---

[17]Cf 1 Tim 5:11-12.

to use it as if it didn't exist, since he says, "Let those who have wives live as though they had none."

So after inserting these words about future things, he returns to the present. Notice that some of his advice concerns the spiritual life (the married woman is anxious about how to please her husband, while the unmarried woman or virgin is anxious about the Lord's affairs), while at other times he argues on the grounds of this present life (I want you to be free from anxieties), but he leaves the choice to them. If he tried to force them to follow the way he has proven to be best, it would look as if he didn't trust his own argument. Instead he tries to hold them in check with gentle persuasion: "I say this for your own benefit, not to lay any restraint upon you, but to promote good order and to secure your undivided devotion to the Lord" (v. 35).

Now, the virgins should listen to what follows: virginity does not simply mean sexual abstinence. She who is anxious about worldly affairs is not really a virgin. In fact, he says that this is the chief difference between a wife and a virgin. He doesn't mention marriage or abstinence, but attachment as opposed to detachment from worldly cares. Sex is not evil, but it is a hindrance to someone who desires to devote all her strength to a life of prayer. "If any one thinks that he is not behaving properly toward his virgin . . ." (v. 36-40). These words refer to a man and a woman living in sexual continence as brother and sister; He approves of this but also says it is no sin if they marry. He concludes the passage by speaking of second marriage after the death of one's spouse. He even allows this, but says that it must be "in the Lord." "In the Lord" means with prudence and decency. We must always pursue these virtues, for without them we will never see God.

No one should accuse me of negligently hurrying through Paul's words about virginity. I have written a whole book about this subject in which I tried to examine accurately every aspect of virginity. It would be a waste of words to bring this topic up again. I refer you to this book if you want a more detailed discussion, and will close with one final statement. We must strive for self-control . . . St Paul tells us to seek peace and the sanctification without which it is impossible to see the Lord. So whether we presently live in virginity, in our first marriage, or in our second, let us pursue holiness, that we may be counted worthy to see Him and to attain the Kingdom of Heaven, through the grace and love for mankind of our Lord Jesus Christ, to whom be glory, dominion, and honor, with the Father and the Holy Spirit, now and ever, and unto ages of ages. Amen.

HOMILY 20
On Ephesians 5:22-33

*Wives, be subject to your husbands, as to the Lord.
For the husband is the head of the wife as Christ
is the head of the Church, His Body, and is Himself
its Savior. As the Church is subject to Christ, so
let wives also be subject in everything to their husbands.*

A certain wise man, when enumerating which blessings
are most important included "a wife and husband who live
in harmony."[1] In another place he emphasized this: "A
friend or a companion never meets one amiss, but a wife
with her husband is better than both."[2] From the beginning
God in His providence has planned this union of man and
woman, and has spoken of the two as one: "male and
female He created them"[3] and "there is neither male nor
female, for you are all one *in Christ Jesus.*"[4] There is no
relationship between human beings so close as that of husband and wife, if they are united as they ought to be. When
blessed David was mourning for Jonathan, who was of one
soul with him, what comparison did he use to describe the
loftiness of their love? "Your love to me was wonderful,
passing the love of women."[5] The power of this love is

---

[1] Sir 25:1.
[2] Sir 40:23.
[3] Gen 1:27.
[4] Gal 3:28.
[5] 2 Sam 1:26.

truly stronger than any passion; other desires may be
strong, but this one alone never fades. This love (eros) is
deeply planted within our inmost being. Unnoticed by us,
it attracts the bodies of men and women to each other,
because in the beginning woman came forth from man, and
from man and woman other men and women proceed.
Can you see now how close this union is, and how God
providentially created it from a single nature? He permitted
Adam to marry Eve, who was more than sister or daughter;
she was his own flesh! God caused the entire human race
to proceed from this one point of origin. He did not, on
the one hand, fashion woman independently from man;
otherwise man would think of her as essentially different
from himself. Nor did He enable woman to bear children
without man; if this were the case she would be self-
sufficient. Instead, just as the branches of a tree proceed
from a single trunk, He made the one man Adam to be
the origin of all mankind, both male and female, and made
it impossible for men and women to be self-sufficient. Later,
He forbade men to marry their sisters or daughters, so that
our love would not be limited to members of our families,
and withdrawn from the rest of the human race. All of this
is implied in Christ's words: "He who made them from
the beginning made them male and female."[6]

The love of husband and wife is the force that welds
society together. Men will take up arms and even sacrifice
their lives for the sake of this love. St Paul would not
speak so earnestly about this subject without serious reason; why else would he say, "Wives, be subject to your
husbands, as to the Lord"? Because when harmony prevails,
the children are raised well, the household is kept in order,
and neighbors, friends and relatives praise the result. Great
benefits, both for families and states, are thus produced.
When it is otherwise, however, everything is thrown into

---

[6]Mt 19:4.

confusion and turned upside-down. When the generals
of an army are at peace with each other, everything
proceeds in an orderly fashion, and when they are not,
everything is in disarray. It is the same here. For the sake of
harmony, then, he said, "Wives, be subject to your husbands
as to the Lord." What? How can He say elsewhere, "Whoever does not renounce wife or husband cannot follow
Me"?[7] If a wife must be subject to her husband as to the
Lord, how can He tell her to separate herself for the Lord's
sake? Indeed she must be subject, but the word "as" does
not always express equivalence. Either Paul means "as
knowing that you are serving the Lord" (which indeed he
says elsewhere, that even if the wife does not obey for her
husband's sake, she must do so primarily for the Lord's
sake); or else he means, "When you yield to your husband,
consider that you are obeying him as part of your service
to the Lord." If "he who resists the authorities (govern-
ments) resists what God has appointed, and those who
resist will incur judgment,"[8] how much more severely will
God judge someone who resists not an external authority,
but that of her own husband, which God has willed from
the beginning?

Let us assume, then, that the husband is to occupy the
place of the head, and the wife that of the body, and listen
to what "headship" means: "For the husband is the head
of the wife as Christ is the head of the Church, His Body,
and is Himself its Savior. As the Church is subject to
Christ, so let wives also be subject in everything to their
husbands." Notice that after saying "the husband is the
head of the wife as Christ is the head of the Church," he
immediately says that the Church is His Body, and He is
Himself its Savior. It is the head that upholds the well-
being of the body. In his other epistles Paul has already laid

---

[7]Cf. Lk 14:33, 18:29.
[8]Rom 13:2.

the foundations of marital love, and has assigned to husband and wife each his proper place: to the husband one of leader and provider, and to the wife one of submission. Therefore as the Church is subject to Christ—and the Church, remember, consists of both husbands and wives—so let wives also be subject in everything to their husbands, as to God.

"Husbands, love your wives, just as Christ also loved the Church" (v. 25). You have heard how important obedience is; you have praised and marvelled at Paul, how he welds our whole life together, as we would expect from an admirable and spiritual man. You have done well. But now listen to what else he requires from you; he has not finished with his example. "Husbands," he says, "love your wives, as Christ loved the Church." You have seen the amount of obedience necessary; now hear about the amount of love necessary. Do you want your wife to be obedient to you, as the Church is to Christ? Then be responsible for the same providential care of her, as Christ is for the Church. And even if it becomes necessary for you to give your life for her, yes, and even to endure and undergo suffering of any kind, do not refuse. Even though you undergo all this, you will never have done anything equal to what Christ has done. You are sacrificing yourself for someone to whom you are already joined, but He offered Himself up for one who turned her back on Him and hated Him. In the same way, then, as He honored her by putting at His feet one who turned her back on Him, who hated, rejected, and disdained Him, as He accomplished this not with threats, or violence, or terror, or anything else like that, but through His untiring love; so also you should behave toward your wife. Even if you see her belittling you, or despising and mocking you, still you will be able to subject her to yourself, through affection, kindness, and your great regard for her. There is no influence more powerful than the bond of love, especially for husband and wife. A servant can be taught submission through fear; but even he, if provoked too much, will soon seek his escape. But one's partner for life, the mother of one's children, the source of one's every joy, should never be fettered with fear and threats, but with love and patience. What kind of marriage can there be when the wife is afraid of her husband? What sort of satisfaction could a husband himself have, if he lives with his wife as if she were a slave, and not with a woman by her own free will? Suffer anything for her sake, but never disgrace her, for Christ never did this with the Church.

He gave Himself up for her that "He might cleanse and sanctify her . . ." (v. 26). So the Church was not pure. She had blemishes, she was ugly and cheap. Whatever kind of wife you marry, you will never take a bride like Christ did when He married the Church; you will never marry anyone estranged from you as the Church was from Christ. Despite all this, He did not abhor or hate her for her extraordinary corruption. Do you want her corruption described? Paul says, "For once you were in darkness."[9] Do you see how black she was? Nothing is blacker than darkness. Think of her shamelessness; she passed her day in malice and envy, Paul says.[10] Look at her impurity; she was foolish and disobedient.[11] But what am I saying? She was foolish, her tongue was evil, but even though her wounds were so numerous, He sacrificed Himself for her in her corrupted state, as if she were in the bloom of youth, as if she were dearly beloved, and a wonderful beauty. St Paul marvelled at this, and said, "Why, one will hardly die for a righteous man—though perhaps for a good man one will dare even to die. But God shows His love for us in that

[9]Eph 5:8.
[10]Tit 3:3.
[11]Idem.

while we were yet sinners Christ died for us."[12] Though she was like this, Christ accepted her and made her beautiful. He washed her, and did not hesitate even to sacrifice Himself for her.

"That He might sanctify her, having cleansed her by the washing of water with the word, that He might present the Church to Himself in splendor, without spot or wrinkle or any such thing, that she might be holy and without blemish" (v. 26-27). "By the washing of water" He washes away her impurities. "With the word" he says. What word? "In the name of the Father and of the Son and of the Holy Spirit."[13] And He has not merely honored her, but He has presented her to Himself in splendor without spot or wrinkle or any such thing. Let us also, then, strive to attain this beauty, and we shall be able to create it within ourselves. Don't expect your wife to have things that are beyond her power. Remember that the Church received everything from her Lord's hands: by Him she was made glorious, by Him she was purified and freed from blemish. Don't turn your back on your wife because she is not beautiful. Listen to what Scripture says: "The bee is small among flying creatures, but her product is the best of sweet things."[14] Your wife is God's creation. If you reproach her, you are not condemning her but Him who made her. What can the woman do about it? If your wife is beautiful, don't praise her for it. Praise, hatred, and even love based on outward beauty come from impure souls. Seek beauty of soul, and imitate the Bridegroom of the Church. Outward beauty is full of conceit and licentiousness; it makes men jealous, and fills men with lustful thought. But does it give any pleasure? Perhaps for one or two months, or a year at most but then no longer;

12Rom 5:7-8.
13Mt 28:19.
14Sir 11:3.

familiarity causes admiration to fade. Meanwhile, the evils arising from outward beauty remain; pride, foolishness, contempt of others. However, where outward beauty is of no concern none of this is to be found. The love that began on honest grounds still continues ardently, since its object is beauty of the soul, not of the body. Just think, what is more beautiful than the sky full of stars? Describe any woman's body you choose, and still there is none so fair; tell me about any eyes you like, yet none are so sparkling. When the stars were created, the very angels gazed in amazement, and we gaze with wonder now; but not with the same amazement as we did when we were children. This is what familiarity does; things no longer strike us in their original intensity. How much more so in the case of a wife! And if by some chance disease comes too, then all is immediately lost. Look for affection, gentleness, and humility in a wife; these are the tokens of beauty. But let us not seek lovely physical features, nor reproach her for lacking things over which she has no control. No; let us not reproach her for anything, or be impatient and sullen. Haven't you seen how many men, living with beautiful wives, have ended their lives in misery, and how many who have lived with those of no great beauty, have lived to extreme old age with great enjoyment? Let us wipe off the "spot" and smooth the "wrinkle" that is within, as it is written; let us do away with the blemishes that are on the soul. Such is the beauty God requires. Let us make her fair in God's sight, not in our own.

Let us not seek wealth, nor high social position (these are external things), but true nobility of soul. Let no one marry a woman for her money; such wealth is base and disgraceful. No, by no means let any one aspire to get rich from his wife. "Those who desire to be rich fall into temptation, into a snare, into many senseless and

hurtful desires that plunge men into ruin and destruction."[15]
Don't look for great wealth in your wife, and you will find
that everything else will go well. Who, tell me, would overlook the most important things to pay attention to secondary matters? And yet, to our sorrow, that is how we behave in practically every case. Yes, if we have a son, we
worry about finding him a rich wife, and not about how
to develop in him a virtuous nature; we worry how he
might acquire money, but not manners. If we engage in
business, we don't think about how it might be free from
sin, but how it might bring in the most profit. Money is
everything now, and so everything has become corrupted
and ruined, because we are possessed by this passion for
money.

"Even so husbands should love their wives as their
own bodies" (v. 28). What does this mean? He is using a
much stronger image and illustration now, much closer and
plainer, and much more demanding. Some might not be
convinced by his previous illustration, saying, "After all,
He was Christ, and Christ is God—naturally He would
sacrifice Himself." Paul's method is different now; he says,
"husbands should love their wives"—because such love is
an obligation, not a favor—"as their own bodies." Why?
"For no man ever hates his own flesh, but nourishes and
cherishes it" (v. 29). That is, he takes particular care of it.
How is she his flesh? Listen: "This at last is bone of my
bones," said Adam, "and flesh of my flesh!"[16] and also,
"They become one flesh."[17] So he nourishes and cherishes
his own flesh, "as Christ does the Church" (v. 29). He
returns here to his first comparison: ". . . because we are
members of His body, of His flesh and of His bones" (v.
30). How is this true? Because Christ was born from our

---

[15]1 Tim 6:9.
[16]Gen 2:23.
[17]Gen 2:24.

Homily 20   51

matter, just as Eve was fashioned from Adam's flesh. Paul
does well here to speak of flesh and bones, for the Lord has
exalted our material substance by partaking of it Himself:
"Since therefore the children share in flesh and blood, He
Himself likewise partook of the same nature."[18] It is
obvious that He shares our nature, but how do we share
His? How are we members of His flesh? We are truly
members of Christ because through Him we were created,
and we are truly members of His flesh because we are
recreated by partaking of His mysteries. There are some
who affirm that He came by water and blood but will not
accept that the Holy Spirit enables us to share His same
essence, through baptism. Foolish heretics! How can the
children who confess His truth and are born again in the
water not become His Body? St Paul explicitly says that
we are members of His flesh and of His bones. Understand
that Adam was fashioned from matter and Christ was born
in the same. From Adam's side came the bearer of corruption, but from Christ's side came life. Death blossomed in
paradise but was slain on the cross. The Son of God shares
our nature so we can share His; as He has us in Him, so
we have Him in us.

"For this reason a man shall leave his father and
mother and be joined to his wife and the two shall become
one flesh" (v. 31). There is another aspect of marital
obligation: Paul shows that a man leaves his parents, who
gave him life, and is joined to his wife, and that one flesh—
father, mother, and child—results from the commingling of
the two. The child is born from the union of their seed, so
the three are one flesh. Our relationship to Christ is the
same; we become one flesh with Him through communion,
more truly one with Him than our children are one with us,
because this has been His plan from the beginning.

Don't make excuses for yourselves; surely you realize

---

[18]Heb 2:14.

that your body has many defects. One person is lame, another has deformed feet or hands, another is sick in one way or other, yet never is anyone so grief-stricken that he cuts off his afflicted member. Instead, he pays more attention to it than to the rest of his body; naturally, since it is part of him. A man should love his spouse as much as he loves himself, not merely because they share the same nature; no, the obligation is far greater, because there are no longer two bodies, but one: he is the head, she the body. Paul says elsewhere, "The head of Christ is God,"[19] and I say that husband and wife are one body in the same way as Christ and the Father are one. Thus we see that the Father is our head also. Paul has combined two illustrations, the natural body and Christ's body; that is why he says, "This is a great mystery, and I take it to mean Christ and the Church" (v. 32). What does this mean? The blessed Moses,—or rather, God—surely reveals in Genesis that for two to become one flesh is a great and wonderful mystery. Now Paul speaks of Christ as the greater mystery; for He left the Father and came down to us, and married His Bride, the Church, and became one spirit with her: "he who is united to the Lord becomes one spirit with Him."[20] Paul says well, "This is a great mystery," as if he were saying, "Nevertheless the allegorical meaning does not invalidate married love." He returns to that subject in what follows.

"However, let each one of you love his wife as himself, and let the wife see that she respects[21] her husband" (v. 33). Indeed, of all actions, it is a mystery, a great mystery indeed, that a man should leave him who gave life to him and brought him up and her who suffered in labor and childbirth. For a man to leave those who have favored him

---

[19] 1 Cor 11:3.
[20] 1 Cor 6:17.
[21] φοβῆται would be more accurately translated, "has in awe."

with so many great blessings, those with whom he has
been in such close contact, and be united to one whom he
has not always known and who often has nothing in common with him, and should honor her more than all others—
that is a mystery indeed. Yet parents are not distressed
when marriages take place, but when they don't! They
are delighted to spend money lavishly on weddings—another
great mystery indeed! And one that contains some hidden
wisdom: Moses prophetically showed this to be so from the
very beginning and Paul proclaims it now, when he compares it to Christ and the Church. This is said not for
the husband's sake alone, however, but for the wife as well,
so that he will cherish his own flesh, as Christ does the
Church, and that she will respect her husband. Paul is no
longer enumerating the duties of love only but of respect
also. The wife is a second authority. She should not demand
equality, for she is subject to the head; neither should the
husband belittle her subjection, for she is the body. If the
head despises the body, it will itself die. Rather, let the
husband counterbalance her obedience with his love. Let
the hands, the feet, and all the rest of the body's parts be
dedicated to the service of the head; but let the head provide for the body, for the head is responsible for all the
members. Nothing can be better than a union like this, but
I know that some will say, "How can there be love where
there is fear?" Most especially there, I say: she who fears,
also loves, and she who loves her husband respects him
because he is her head. Also, she loves him because he is
a part of her body, since the head is a member of the body
as well. Paul places the head in authority and the body in
obedience for the sake of peace. Where there is equal
authority, there never is peace. A household cannot be a
democracy, ruled by everyone, but the authority must
necessarily rest in one person. The same is true for the
Church: when men are led by the Spirit of Christ, then
there is peace. There were five thousand men in the Jeru-

salem church, and they were of one heart and soul, and
no one said that any of the things which he possessed was
his own,[22] but they were subject to one another; this surely
is an illustration of wisdom and godly fear. Notice, however,
that Paul explains love in detail, comparing it to Christ's
love for the Church and our love for our own flesh, saying
that for this reason a man leaves his father and mother,
but he does not elaborate concerning fear. Why so?
He would much prefer love to prevail, because where
there is love, everything else follows, but where love
is absent, fear will be of no use. If a man loves his wife,
he will bear with her even when she isn't very obedient.
How difficult it is to have harmony when husband and wife
are not bound together by the power of love! Fear is no
substitute for this. That is why he speaks at greater length
about the stronger force. So if you think that the wife is
the loser because she is told to fear her husband, remember
that the principal duty of love is assigned to the husband,
and you will see that it is her gain. "And what if my wife
refuses to obey me?" a husband will ask. Never mind!
Your obligation is to love her; do your duty! Even when
we don't receive our due from others, we must always do
our duty. Here is an example: Paul begins this passage by
saying, "Be subject to one another out of reverence for
Christ." If your spouse doesn't obey God's law, you are
not excused. A wife should respect her husband even when
he shows her no love, and a husband should love his wife
even when she shows him no respect. Then they will both
be found to lack nothing, since each has fulfilled the
commandment given to him.

This, then, is what it means to marry in Christ: spiritual
marriage is like spiritual birth, which is not of blood, nor
of the will of the flesh.[23] Consider the birth of Isaac; Scrip-

---

[22]Acts 4:32.
[23]Cf Jn 1:13.

ture says, "It had ceased to be with Sarah after the manner of women."[24] Her marriage was not one of fleshly passion, but wholly spiritual, just as the soul is joined to God in an ineffable union which He alone knows: "He who is united to the Lord becomes one spirit with Him."[25] See how he does not despise physical unity, however, but uses spiritual unity to illustrate it! How foolish are those who belittle marriage! If marriage were something to be condemned, Paul would never call Christ a bridegroom and the Church a bride, and then say this is an illustration of a man leaving his father and his mother, and again refer to Christ and the Church. The Psalmist prophesies of the Church when he says, "Hear, O daughter, consider, and incline your ear; forget your people and your father's house, and the king will desire your beauty,"[26] and the Gospel says concerning Christ: "I came from the Father and have come into the world."[27] When it says that Christ "left" the Father, don't imagine that there was a change of place, as there is with people. "I came" is not to be understood in terms of motion, but in reference to the incarnation.

Why does Paul speak of the husband being joined to the wife, but not of the wife to the husband? Since he is describing the duties of love, he addresses the man. He speaks to the woman concerning respect, saying that the husband is the head of the wife, as Christ is the head of the Church; but to the husband he speaks of love, and obliges him to love, and tells him how he should love, thus binding and cementing him to his wife. If a man leaves his father for his wife's sake, and then abandons her for whose sake he left his father, what pardon can he deserve? Do you not see, husband, the great honor that God desires

---

[24]Gen 18:11.
[25]1 Cor 6:17.
[26]Ps 45:10-11.
[27]Jn 16:28.

you to give your wife? He has taken you from your father
and bound[28] you to her. How can a believing husband say
that he has no obligation if his spouse disobeys him? Paul
is lenient only when an unbeliever wishes to separate: "But
if the unbelieving partner desires to separate, let it be so;
in such a case the brother or sister is not bound."[29] And
when you hear Paul say "fear" or "respect," ask for the
respect due you from a free woman, not the fear you
would demand from a slave. She is your body; if you do
this, you dishonor yourself by dishonoring your own body.
What does this "respect" entail? She should not stubbornly
contradict you, and not rebel against your authority as if
she were the head of the house; this is enough. If you desire greater respect, you must love as you are commanded.
Then there will be no need for fear; love itself will accomplish everything. The female sex is rather weak and needs
a lot of support, a lot of condescension. I am not condemning those who are joined in second marriages. God forbid!
The Apostle Paul himself permits them, though indeed he
does so as a concession. Provide your wife with everything
and endure troubles for her sake; you are obliged to do so.
Here Paul does not think it appropriate to illustrate his
point with outside sources, as he does in so many other
cases. The wisdom of Christ, so great and forceful, is
sufficient, especially in the matter of the wife's subjection.
"A man shall leave his father and mother," he says; but
he does not say, "he shall dwell with," but instead, "he shall
cling" to his wife, thus demonstrating the closeness of the
union, and the sincerity of the love. And Paul is not satisfied even with this, but goes further, explaining the subjection of the wife in the context of the two being no longer
two. He does not say "one spirit" or "one soul" (union like
this is possible for anyone), but he says "one flesh." The

---

[28]Προσήλωσε = nailed.
[29]1 Cor 7:15.

wife is a secondary authority, but nevertheless she possesses
real authority and equality of dignity while the husband
still retains the role of headship; the welfare of the household is thus maintained. Paul uses the example of Christ
to show that we should not only love but also govern, "that
she might be holy and without blemish." The word "flesh"
and the phrase "shall cling" both refer to love, and making
her "holy and without blemish" refer to headship. Do both
these things, and everything else will follow. Seek the
things which please God, and those which please man will
follow soon enough. Instruct your wife, and your whole
household will be in order and harmony. Listen to what
Paul says: "If there is anything they desire to know, let them
ask their husbands at home."[30] If we regulate our households in this way, we will also be fit to oversee the Church,
for indeed the household is a little Church. Therefore, it is
possible for us to surpass all others in virtue by becoming
good husbands and wives.

Consider Abraham and Sarah, and Isaac, and the three
hundred eighteen men born in his house.[31] That household
was united in harmony and piety, a perfect illustration of
the apostolic precept. Sarah respected her husband; listen
to her words: "It has not yet happened to me, and I am
old, and my lord is old also."[32] He loved her in return and
always did what she asked. Their son was virtuous, and
their servants were so loyal that they willingly risked their
lives for their master, without asking why. The chief
servant was so admirable that he was entrusted with ar-
ranging Isaac's marriage, and had to go away on a long
journey. As with a general whose troops are so well organ-
ized on the front that the enemy cannot find a place to pene-
trate for an attack, so it is with husband and wife: when

---

[30] 1 Cor 14:35.
[31] Gen 14:14.
[32] Gen 18:12 (LXX).

the concerns of everyone in the house are the same, harmony reigns in the family, but if not, the entire household is easily broken up and destroyed.

Let us therefore painstakingly care for our wives and children. By doing so, we are making our obligation of headship an easy task. Thus we will have a good defense before Christ's judgment seat, and will be able to say, "Behold, I and the children whom the Lord has given me are signs and portents in Israel."[33] If the husband is admirable and the head sound, then the rest of the body will suffer no harm. Paul has precisely described for husband and wife what is fitting behavior for each: she should reverence him as the head and he should love her as his body. But how is this behavior achieved? That it must be is clear; now I will tell you how. It will be achieved if we are detached from money, if we strive above everything for virtue, if we keep the fear of God before our eyes. What Paul says to servants in the next chapter applies to us as well, ". . . knowing that whatever good anyone does, he will receive the same again from the Lord."[34] Love her not so much for her own sake, but for Christ's sake. That is why he says, "be subject . . . as to the Lord." Do everything for the Lord's sake, in a spirit of obedience to Him. These words should be enough to convince us to avoid quarrels and disagreements. No husband should believe any accusation he hears from a third party about his wife, and vice versa; nor should a wife unreasonably monitor her husband's comings and goings, provided that he has always shown himself to be above suspicion. And what if you devote the day to your work and your friends, and the evening to your wife; but she is still not satisfied, but is jealous for more of your time? Don't be annoyed by her complaints; she loves you, she is not behaving absurdly—

---

[33]Is 18:8.
[34]Eph 6:8.

her complains come from her fervent affection for you, and from fear. Yes, she is afraid that her marriage bed will be stolen, that someone will deprive her of her greatest blessing, that someone will take from her him who is her head.

When you are tempted to jealousy, think again of Abraham and Sarah's household. While Sarah was still barren, she herself asked Abraham to take her maid Hagar as a concubine. It was her idea alone; Abraham had not so much as suggested it, though they were childless in their old age. He chose to be a father rather than to grieve his wife, yet after all this, what did Sarah say to him once Hagar had conceived? "May the wrong done to me be on you! May the Lord judge between you and me!"[35] Now if he had been anyone else, would he not have been moved to anger? Would he not have said to her, "What do you mean? I had no desire to have anything to do with the woman; it was all your doing, and are you now blaming me?" No, he said nothing of the sort, but only, "Behold your maid is in your power; do to her as you please."[36] He gave up the woman who had shared his bed, who had therefore become one flesh with him, so as not to grieve Sarah; surely he must have valued his wife above everything. More than this, Hagar was bearing his child. What man would not pity a woman who had just conceived his own son? But righteous Abraham was unmoved, and put nothing before the love he owed his wife. Let us imitate his patience.

A wife should never nag her husband: "You lazy coward, you have no ambition! Look at our relatives and neighbors; they have plenty of money. Their wives have far more than I do." Let no wife say any such thing; she is her husband's body, and it is not for her to dictate to her head, but to submit and obey. "But why should she

---

[35]Gen 16:5.
[36]Gen 16:6.

endure poverty?" some will ask. If she is poor, let her console herself by thinking of those who are much poorer still. If she really loved her husband, she would never speak to him like that, but would value having him close to her more than all the gold in the world. Likewise, if a husband has a wife who behaves this way, he must never exercise his authority by insulting and abusing her. Instead, he should show true nobility of spirit, and patiently remind her that in the wisdom of heaven, poverty is no evil. Then she will stop complaining. But he must not teach her only by words, but by deeds. He should teach her to be detached from high social position. If he is so himself, she will imitate him. Beginning on their wedding night, let him be an example of gentleness, temperance, and self-control; and she will be likewise. He should advise her not to decorate herself with golden earrings, necklaces, or other jewelry, or to accumulate expensive clothes. Instead, her appearance should be dignified, and dignity is never served by theatrical excess. Furnish your house neatly and soberly. If the bridegroom shows his wife that he takes no pleasure in worldly excess, and will not stand for it, their marriage will remain free from the evil influences that are so popular these days. Let them shun the immodest music and dancing that are currently so fashionable. I am aware that many people think me ridiculous for giving such advice; but if you listen to me, you will understand the advantages of a sober life-style more and more as time goes on. You will no longer laugh at me, but will laugh instead at the way people live now like silly children or drunken men. What is our duty, then? Remove from your lives shameful, immodest, and Satanic music, and don't associate with people who enjoy such profligate entertainment. When your bride sees your manner of life, she will say to herself, "Wonderful! What a wise man my husband is! He regards this passing life as nothing; he has married me to be a good mother for his children and a prudent manager of his household." Will this sort of life be distasteful for a young bride? Only perhaps for the shortest time, and soon she will discover how delightful it is to live this way. She will retain her modesty if you retain yours. Don't engage in idle conversations; it never profits anyone to talk too much. Whenever you give your wife advice, always begin by telling her how much you love her. Nothing will persuade her so well to admit the wisdom of your words as her assurance that you are speaking to her with sincere affection. Tell her that you are convinced that money is not important, that only thieves thirst for it constantly, that you love her more than gold; and indeed an intelligent, discreet, and pious young woman is worth more than all the money in the world. Tell her that you love her more than your own life, because this present life is nothing, and that your only hope is that the two of you pass through this life in such a way that in the world to come you will be united in perfect love. Say to her, "Our time here is brief and fleeting, but if we are pleasing to God, we can exchange this life for the Kingdom to come. Then we will be perfectly one both with Christ and each other, and our pleasure will know no bounds. I value your love above all things, and nothing would be so bitter or painful to me as our being at odds with each other. Even if I lose everything, any affliction is tolerable if you will be true to me." Show her that you value her company, and prefer being at home to being out. Esteem her in the presence of your friends and children. Praise and show admiration for her good acts; and if she ever does anything foolish, advise her patiently. Pray together at home and go to Church; when you come back home, let each ask the other the meaning of the readings and the prayers. If you are overtaken by poverty, remember Peter and Paul, who were more honored than kings or rich men, though they spent their lives in hunger and thirst. Remind one another that nothing in life is to be feared, except offending God. If your marriage is like this, your perfection will rival the holiest of monks.

If you are inclined to entertain and give dinner parties, there should be nothing immodest or excessive about them. And if you should find some poor, saintly man who just by stepping into your house would bring God's blessing upon you, invite him. Now I'll add one more thing: none of you should look for a rich woman to marry, but a poor one instead. You'll get no satisfaction from her money, since if she is rich she will annoy you with her taunts and demands. She'll be disrespectful and extravagant, and will frustrate you by saying things like, "Don't complain about all my clothes! I haven't spent anything of yours; I'm still wearing my own clothes bought with the inheritance my parents gave me." What are you saying, woman? Still wearing your own clothes? What can be worse than this sort of language? You no longer have a body of your own (since you gave it away in marriage), yet you have money of your own? After marriage, you are no longer two, but one flesh, and are your possessions still divided? Love of money! You have both become one person, one organism, and can you still say, "my own"? This cursed and abominable phrase comes from the devil. Things far nearer and dearer to us than material possessions God has made common to all: we can't say "my own light, my own sun, my own water." If all our greater blessings are held in common, why should money not be? Let the riches be lost ten thousand times over! Or rather let not the riches be lost, but that frame of mind that doesn't know how to use money, but holds it higher in esteem than all other things.

Teach her these lessons along with the others I have indicated, but do it with much compassion. The virtuous life has in itself much that is difficult to follow, so whenever you have to lecture her on the meaning of true wisdom, be sure that you humble yourself and that your words are full of grace and kindness. Above all, remove from her soul this notion of "mine" and "yours." If she says the word "mine," ask her, "What things do you call yours? I honestly don't know what you mean; for my part, I have nothing of my own. How can you speak of 'mine' when everything is yours? I am yours!" These words aren't meant to flatter her, but they are full of wisdom and will soothe her anger, and end her disappointment. It is flattery when a man acts dishonorably with an evil motive in mind; this, however, is the most honorable of motives. When you say, "I am yours," you are repeating St Paul's own advice: "For the wife does not rule over her own body, but the husband does; likewise the husband does not rule over his own body, but the wife does."[37] Say also, "If I have no power over my own body, but rather you do, how much more power is yours over my material possessions?" By speaking this way you will put the devil to shame, and will firmly unite her to yourself. Thus you will teach her, by your own manner of speaking, never to speak in terms of "mine" and "yours."

Finally, never call her by her name alone, but with terms of endearment, honor, and love. If you honor her, she won't need honor from others; she won't desire praise from others if she enjoys the praise that comes from you. Prefer her before all others, both for her beauty and her discernment, and praise her. She will in this way be persuaded to listen to none that are outside, but to disregard all the world except for you. Teach her to fear God, and all other good things will flow from this one lesson as from a fountain and your house will be filled with ten thousand blessings. If we seek the things that are perfect, the secondary things will follow. The Lord says, "Seek first the kingdom of God and His righteousness, and all these things shall be added to you."[38] What sort of person do you think the children of such parents will be? What

[37]1 Cor 7:4.
[38]Mt 6:33.

kind of person are all the others who associate with them? Will they not eventually be the recipients of countless blessings as well? For generally the children acquire the character of their parents, are formed in the mold of their parents' temperament, love the same things their parents love, talk in the same fashion, and work for the same ends. If we order our lives in this way and diligently study the Scriptures, we will find lessons to guide us in everything we need! In this way we will be able to please God, and to pass through the course of this life in virtue and to gain those blessings which He has promised to those who love Him, of which, God willing, may we be counted worthy through the grace and love for mankind of our Lord Jesus Christ, with whom, together with the Holy Spirit, be glory, honor, and power to the Father, now and ever, and unto ages of ages. Amen.

HOMILY 21
On Ephesians 6:1-4

Children, obey your parents in the Lord, for this is right. "Honor your father and your mother" (this is the first commandment with a promise) "that it may be well with you and that you may live long on the earth." (Eph 6:1-3)

St Paul develops his theme in an orderly fashion: he has spoken first concerning the husband, then the wife, who is second authority; now he proceeds to the next rank, namely the children. The husband is the head of the wife, and husband and wife together have authority over the children. Listen to what he says: "Children, obey your parents in the Lord, for this is the first commandment with a promise." He will not speak here about Christ, or other lofty subjects, but will direct his words to young minds; that is also why this passage is very short, since children have a short span of attention. Nor does he speak here about the kingdom to come, since children would not be able to understand, but he tells what a child's soul wants to hear most—how to have a long life. If anyone wonders why he doesn't speak about the kingdom of God, but simply gives them the Old Testament commandment, it is because he addresses the children on their own level, and because he is well aware that if husband and wife order their lives according to God's law, their children will also submit willingly to the same law. The most difficult element

65

in any undertaking is to lay a good strong foundation, based on sound principles; anything begun this way will easily proceed to the proper conclusion. "Children," he says, "obey your parents in the Lord," that is to say, *in accordance with* the Lord, for so has God commanded you.

"What if my parents command me to do things that are wrong?" you might ask. Well, even when a parent does wicked things himself, he usually doesn't force his children to imitate him. However, St Paul has left us a provision in this case, by saying, "Obey your parents *in the Lord*," that is, whenever they tell you to do what is pleasing to God. So if your father is an unbeliever, or a heretic, and demands that you follow him, you ought not to obey, because what he commands is not in the Lord.

Now why does St Paul say that this commandment is the first to be joined with a promise? Notice that the other commandments, such as "Thou shalt not kill," or "Thou shalt not commit adultery," have no reward attached to them, since God gave these commandments to make us avoid *evil* things. But the commandment to honor our parents concerns something *good,* so a reward is promised for those who keep it. See what an admirable foundation St Paul lays for a virtuous life: honor and respect for one's parents. This is the first good practice commanded us in the Scriptures, because before all others, except God, our parents are the authors of our life, and they deserve to be the first ones to receive the fruits of our good deeds. Only after we honor our parents can we do anything good for the rest of mankind. If a man does not honor his parents, he will never treat other people with kindness.

He has given the children the most important advice, so he continues by saying to the fathers: "Fathers, do not provoke your children to anger, but bring them up in the discipline and instruction of the Lord" (v. 4). He does not say, "love them." He would regard such a commandment as superfluous, trusting that nature will draw even un-

willing parents to the love of their children. What does he
say? "Do not provoke your children to anger," as many by
disinheriting and disowning them, or by overburdening them,
as if they were slaves and not free. But most importantly,
he shows that the father, as the head and source of authority in the family, is responsible for leading his children to
obedience. As the wife must submit to her husband, and
the husband must make himself worthy of her obedience
by the power of love, likewise he must also "bring his
children up in the discipline and instruction of the Lord."
Concern for spiritual things will unite the family. Do you
want your child to be obedient? Then from the beginning
bring him up in the discipline and instruction of the Lord.
Don't think that it isn't necessary for a child to listen to
the Scriptures; the first thing he will hear from them will
be, "Honor your father and your mother," and immediately
you will begin to reap your reward. Don't say, "Bible-
reading is for monks; am I turning my child into a monk?"
No! It isn't necessary for him to be a monk. Make him
into a Christian! Why are you afraid of something so good?
It is necessary for everyone to know Scriptural teachings,
and this is especially true for children. Even at their age
they are exposed to all sorts of folly and bad examples from
popular entertainments. Our children need remedies for all
these things! We are so concerned with our children's
schooling; if only we were equally zealous in bringing
them up in the discipline and instruction of the Lord! And
then we wonder why we reap such bitter fruit when we
have raised our children to be insolent, licentious, impious,
and vulgar. May this never happen; instead, let us heed
the blessed Paul's admonition to bring them up in the
discipline and instruction of the Lord. Let us give them a
pattern to imitate; from their earliest years let us teach
them to study the Bible. "He repeats this over and over
again," you say; "we are sick of listening to it." Never
will I stop doing my duty! Why do you refuse to imitate

the holy men and women of old? Tell me! Especially you
mothers: think of Hannah's example; look at what she
did. She brought Samuel, her only son, to the temple, when
he was only an infant! Who among you would not rather
have a son like Samuel than one who became king of the
whole world ten thousand times over? "But it's impossible,"
you say, "for my son ever to become as great as he." Why
is it impossible? Because you *don't* really want it; you won't
entrust him to the One who is able to make him great. And
who is that? God. Hannah commended Samuel into the
hands of God. The high priest Eli had no real ability to
form him, since he even failed to form his own children.
It was the mother's faith and zeal that made everything
possible. He was her first and only child. She didn't know
if she would ever have another, yet she never said, "I'll
wait until he grows up; he should have a taste of worldly
pleasures, during his childhood at least." No; she rejected
all these thoughts, for she had only one object: how from
the very beginning she could dedicate her heart's delight to
God. Be ashamed, you men, at the wisdom of this woman.
She gave Samuel to God, and with God she left him, and
thus her marriage was blessed more than ever, because her
first concern was for spiritual things. She dedicated the
first-fruits of her womb to God and obtained many more
children in return. She saw Samuel honored even in this
life. If men return honor for honor, will not God do much
more? He gives so much even to those who don't honor
Him at all! How long are we to be mere lumps of flesh?
How long will we cling to the ground? Let everything take
second place to our care for our children, our bringing
them up in the discipline and instruction of the Lord. If
from the beginning we teach them to love true wisdom,
they will have greater wealth and glory than riches can
provide. If a child learns a trade, or is highly educated for
a lucrative profession, all this is nothing compared to the
art of detachment from riches; if you want to make your

child rich, teach him this. He is truly rich who does not desire great possessions, or surround himself with wealth, but who requires nothing. This is how to discipline and teach your child; this is the greatest riches. Don't worry about giving him an influential reputation for worldly wisdom, but ponder deeply how you can teach him to think lightly of this life's passing glories; thus he will become truly renowned and glorious. Whether you are poor or rich, you can do this; these lessons are not learned from a skillful professor, but from divine revelation. Don't ask how he can enjoy a long life here, but how he can enjoy an infinite and eternal life in the age to come. Give him the great things, not the little things. Don't strive to make him a clever orator, but teach him to love true wisdom. He will not suffer if he lacks clever words; but if he lacks wisdom, all the rhetoric in the world can't help him. A pattern of life is what is needed, not empty speeches; character, not cleverness; deeds, not words. These things will secure the Kingdom and bestow God's blessings. Don't sharpen his tongue, but purify his soul. I don't mean that worldly learning is worthless and to be ignored, but it should not be an exclusive preoccupation. Don't think that only monks need to learn the Bible; children about to go out into the world stand in greater need of Scriptural knowledge. A man who never travels by sea doesn't need to know how to equip a ship, or where to find a pilot or a crew, but a sailor has to know all these things. The same applies to the monk and the man of this world. The monk lives an untroubled life in a calm harbor, removed from every storm, while the worldly man is always sailing the ocean, battling innumerable tempests.

Would you like me to give examples of men whose lives were patterns of virtue, even though they lived in the world? These days we have none to compare with them, even among the righteous. I am referring to the holy men of the Old Testament. How many of them had wives and

children, yet were in no way inferior to the greatest ascetic?
Now, unfortunately, because of the present distress this is
no longer the case; as the blessed Paul has said.[1] Of which
of them should I speak? Noah, or Abraham? The son of
one, or of the other? Or Joseph? What about the prophets,
such as Moses, or Isaiah? If you will permit me, I will speak
of Abraham, who in many ways is the greatest example of
them all. Was he not married? Did he not have children?
Yes, but these things in themselves did not make him
remarkable. He was rich; but it was not his riches that
made him pleasing to God. Why is he called wonderful?
Because of his hospitality, his detachment from riches, and
his well-ordered life. What makes a lover of wisdom? Does
he not care little for wealth or fame? Does he not rise
above envy and other evil passions? Consider what a lover
of true wisdom Abraham was. First, he was not attached
to his homeland. God said: "Go from your country and
your kindred and your father's house . . ."[2] and immediately he went. He wasn't tied down to his house, (or he
never would have left it), or his friends, or anything else,
least of all money and fame. When he had defeated the
four kings, and was invited to take the spoil, he refused it.[3]

All these great men looked at this present life as
nothing; they did not thirst for riches or other earthly
attachments. Tell me, which trees are best? Do we not
prefer those that are inwardly strong, and are not injured
by rainstorms, or hail, or gusts of wind, or by any sort of
harsh weather, but stand exposed to them all without fences
or garden to protect them? He who truly loves wisdom is
like this, and his riches we have already described. He has
nothing, yet has everything; he has everything, yet has
nothing. A fence does not provide internal strength, nor

---

[1] 1 Cor 7:26.
[2] Gen 12:1.
[3] Cf Gen 14:17ff.

is a wall a natural support; they provide only artificial protection. What is a strong body? Is it not one that is healthy, whether hungry or surfeited, cold or warm? Or is it something that is dependent on restaurants, tailors, merchants, and physicians for health? The truly rich man, the true lover of wisdom, needs none of these things, and that is why the blessed apostle admonishes us to bring our children up in the discipline and instruction of the Lord. Don't surround them with the external safeguards of wealth and fame, for when these fail—and they will fail—our children will stand naked and defenseless, having gained no profit from their former prosperity, but only injury, since when those artificial protections that shielded them from the winds are removed, they will be blown to the ground in a moment.

Therefore wealth is a hindrance, because it leaves us unprepared for the hardships of life. So, let us raise our children in such a way that they can face any trouble, and not be surprised when difficulties come; let us bring them up in the discipline and instruction of the Lord. Great will be the reward in store for us, for if artists who make statues and paint portraits of kings are held in high esteem, will not God bless ten thousand times more those who reveal and beautify His royal image (for man is the image of God)? When we teach our children to be good, to be gentle, to be forgiving (all these are attributes of God), to be generous, to love their fellow men, to regard this present age as nothing, we instill virtue in their souls, and reveal the image of God within them. This, then, is our task: to educate both ourselves and our children in godliness; otherwise what answer will we have before Christ's judgment-seat? If a man with unruly children is unworthy to be a bishop,[4] how can he be worthy of the kingdom of heaven? What do you think? If we have an undisciplined

---

4Cf Tit 1:6.

wife, or unruly children, shall we not have to render an account for them? Yes, we shall if we cannot offer to God what we owe Him, because we can't be saved through individual righteousness alone. If the man who buried his one talent gained nothing, but was punished instead, it is obvious that one's own virtue is not enough for salvation, but the virtue of those for whom we are responsible is also required. Therefore, let us be greatly concerned for our wives and our children, and for ourselves as well, and as we educate both ourselves and them let us beg God to help us in our task. If He sees that we care about this, He will help us; but if we are unconcerned. He will not give us His hand. God helps those who work, not those who are idle. No one helps an inactive person, but one who joins in the labor. The good God Himself will bring this work to perfection, so that all of us may be counted worthy of the blessings He has promised, through the grace and love for mankind of His Son Jesus Christ our Lord, with whom, together with the Holy Spirit, be glory, honor and power to the Father, now and ever, and unto ages of ages. Amen.

HOMILY 12
On Colossians 4:18

I, Paul, write this greeting with my own hand. Remember my bonds. Grace be with you. Amen.

Paul concludes his epistle to the Colossians with these words, so that they will not be afraid for him. He tells them that even though he, their teacher, is in chains, his soul is free through grace. Even his imprisonment is an act of grace. Listen to what Luke says in the Acts of the Apostles: "The apostles left the presence of the council, rejoicing that they were counted worthy to suffer dishonor for the Name."[1] If a man willingly suffers for his wife, whom he loves, how much more willingly should we suffer for Christ? So never be distressed about the tribulations you endure for Christ's sake. Remember Paul's bonds, and you will be encouraged. Are you proud of your good deeds? Remember Paul's bonds, and you will see how unreasonable it is for you to be surrounded with pleasures, while his life was continually endangered. Does your heart crave self-indulgence? Think of Paul in prison. You are his disciple, his fellow-soldier. How can you want to live in luxury, while your fellow-soldier is in chains? Has everyone in this world forsaken you? Remember Paul in prison, and understand that to be alone is not to be forsaken. Do you delight in expensive clothes, or golden jewelry? Remember Paul's bonds, and these things will seem to you as more worthless

[1]Acts 5:41.

than a prostitute's filthy rags, or a handful of withered grass. Do you spend long hours adorning your hair, and painting your face with cosmetics, hoping to make yourself beautiful? Think of Paul's squalor in prison, and you will burn with desire for his beauty. You will then consider worldly beauty to be ugly, and will bitterly long to share Paul's chains. Think of his face streaming with tears. Day and night for three years he never ceased his weeping.[2] Imitate his weeping. Make your face bright with tears. Weep for your sins: your anger, your loss of self-control, your love of revelry. Imitate Paul's tears, and you will laugh to scorn the vanities of this passing life. Christ blessed these tears,when He said, "Blessed are you that weep now, for you shall laugh."[3] Nothing is sweeter than these tears; they are more to be desired than any laughter. Pray earnestly for these tears, so that when others sin, your heart may be broken for them. Raise your sons and daughters in the same way; weep for them when you see them led astray. Remember the psalmist's words: "The Lord has heard the sound of my weeping; the Lord accepts my prayer."[4]

"Remember my bonds," Paul says. Marriage is a bond, a bond ordained by God. Why then do you celebrate weddings in a silly and immodest manner? Have you no idea what you are doing? You are marrying your wife for the procreation of children and for moderation of life; what is the meaning of these drunken parties with their lewd and disgraceful behavior? You can enjoy a banquet with your friends to celebrate your marriage; I do not forbid this, but why must you introduce all these excesses? Camels and mules behave more decently than some people at wedding receptions! Is marriage a comedy? It is a mystery, an image

---

2Cf Acts 20:31.
3Lk 6:21.
4Ps 6:8, 9.

of something far greater. If you have no respect for marriage, at least respect what it symbolizes: "This is a great mystery, and I take it to mean Christ and the Church."[5] It is an image of the Church, and of Christ, and will you celebrate in a profane manner? "But then who will dance?" you ask. Why does anyone need to dance? Pagan mysteries are the only ones that involve dancing. We celebrate our mysteries quietly and decently, with reverence and modesty. How is marriage a mystery? The two have become one. This is not an empty symbol. They have not become the image of anything on earth, but of God Himself. How can you celebrate it with a noisy uproar, which dishonors and bewilders the soul?

They come to be made into one body. See the mystery of love! If the two do not become one, they cannot increase; they can increase only by decreasing! How great is the strength of unity! God's ingenuity in the beginning divided one flesh into two; but He wanted to show that it remained one even after its division, so He made it impossible for either half to procreate without the other. Now do you see how great a mystery marriage is? From one man, Adam, he made Eve; then He reunited these two into one, so that their children would be produced from a single source. Likewise, husband and wife are not two, but one; if he is the head and she is the body, how can they be two? She was made from his side; so they are two halves of one organism. God calls her a "helper" to demonstrate their unity, and He honors the unity of husband and wife above that of child and parents. A father rejoices to see his son or daughter marry; it is as if his child's body is finally becoming complete. Even though he spends so much money for his daughter's wedding, he would rather do that than see her remain unmarried, since

[5]Eph 5:32.

then she would seem to be deprived of her own flesh. We are not sufficient unto ourselves in this life.

How do they become one flesh? As if she were gold receiving the purest of gold, the woman receives the man's seed with rich pleasure, and within her it is nourished, cherished, and refined. It is mingled with her own substance and she then returns it as a child! The child is a bridge connecting mother to father, so the three become one flesh, as when two cities divided by a river are joined by a bridge. And here that bridge is formed from the substance of each! Just as the head and the rest of the body are one, since the neck connects but does not divide them, so it is with the child. That is why Scripture does not say, "They shall be one flesh," but that they shall be joined together "into one flesh,"[6] namely the child. But suppose there is no child; do they then remain two and not one? No; their intercourse effects the joining of their bodies, and they are made one, just as when perfume is mixed with ointment.

I know that my words embarrass many of you, and the reason for your shame is your own wanton licentiousness. "Let marriage be held in honor among all, and let the marriage bed be undefiled,"[7] yet you give marriage a bad name with your depraved celebrations. Why else would you be ashamed at what is honorable, or blush at what is undefiled? That is why I want to purify your wedding celebrations: to restore marriage to its due nobility and to silence those heretics who call it evil. God's gift is insulted. It is the root of our very existence, and we smother it with dung and filth. This is what I want to wash away by my words. So listen to me a little while longer. Remember that you can't cling to filth without picking up the stench. Some of you call my words immodest, because I speak of the nature of marriage, which is honorable; yet

---

[6]Gen 2:24 (LXX).
[7]Heb 13:4.

you show no modesty in your behavior at weddings. By calling my words immodest, you condemn God, who is the author of marriage. Shall I also tell you how marriage is a mystery of the Church? The Church was made from the side of Christ, and He united Himself to her in a spiritual intercourse. St Paul says, "I betrothed you to Christ to present you as a pure virgin to her one husband,"[8] and "we are members of His body, of His flesh, and of His bones."[9] Think about all this and stop treating such a great mystery so shamefully. Marriage is an image of the presence of Christ, and will you get drunk at a wedding? Tell me, if you saw a portrait of the emperor, would you insult it? By no means.

Many are indifferent to what goes on at wedding celebrations, but great evil is the result. Looseness and disorder prevail. Paul says, "Let there be no filthiness, nor silly talk, nor levity; let no evil talk come out of your mouths."[10] What, I ask you, goes on at weddings? All of this, and more, for evil talk has become an art, and those who excel in it are applauded! Sins have become an art! We pursue them not by chance, but with studied earnestness, and finally the devil assumes control of his own troops. When drunkenness arrives, chastity departs. Where there is filthy talk, the devil is always eager to make his own contribution. Do you celebrate Christ's mystery with entertainment like this, by inviting the devil? I am sure now that I have offended you. You mock me when I rebuke you, and say I am too austere. This is only another proof of your perverted manner of life. Don't you remember St Paul's words: "So, whether you eat or drink, or whatever you do, do all to the glory of God"? Or the Psalmist's, when

he said, "Serve the Lord with fear and rejoice in him with
trembling"?[12] But your behavior is dishonorable and
blasphemous, totally without restraint. Is it not possible
for pleasure and temperance to co-exist? Are you fond of
music? I would prefer that you love silence best of all, but
if you must have songs, choose edifying ones, not satanic
ones. Instead of dancing girls, invite the choir of angels
to your wedding. "But how can we see them?" you ask.
If you drive away the other things, Christ Himself will
come to your wedding, and where Christ goes, the angels'
choir follows. If you ask Him, He will work for you an
even greater miracle than He worked in Cana: that is, He
will transform the water of your unstable passions into
the wine of spiritual unity, but remember: if He should
come and find the musicians and the crowd making a
tumult, He will expel them all before working His wonders.[13] What is more disgusting than these pomps of the
devil? There is so much noise that nothing can be heard.
When any words are audible, they are meaningless, shameful, and disgusting.

There is nothing more pleasurable than virtue, nothing
sweeter than orderliness, nothing more honorable than
dignity. Those who celebrate weddings such as this will
find true pleasure, but pay attention now to what is required
for such a marriage. First, look for a husband who will
really be a husband and a protector; remember that you
are placing a head on a body. When your daughter is to
be married, don't look for how much money a man has.
Don't worry about his nationality or his family's social
position. All these things are superfluous. Look instead
for piety, gentleness, wisdom, and the fear of the Lord,
if you want your daughter to be happy. If you insist on
her marrying a wealthy man, you are hurting her, not

[12]Ps 2:11.
[13]Cf Mt 9:23ff.

helping her. He will treat her like a slave because she comes from a family poorer than his. Instead, she should marry a man whose financial condition is the same as hers, or even one who is poorer—that is, if your desire is to give your daughter to a husband, and not to sell her as a slave to a master. When you are satisfied that the man is virtuous, and decide what day they will be married, beseech Christ to be present at the wedding. He is not ashamed to come, for marriage is an image of His presence in the Church. Even better than this: pray that your children will each find such a virtuous spouse; entrust this concern of yours into His hands. If you honor Him in this way, He will return honor for honor.

When you prepare for the wedding, don't run to your neighbors' houses borrowing extra mirrors, or spend endless hours worrying about dresses. A wedding is not a pageant or a theatrical performance. Instead, make your house as beautiful as you can, and then invite your family and your neighbors and friends. Invite as many people as you know that have good character, and they will be content with what you set before them. Don't hire bands or orchestras; such an expense is excessive and unbecoming. Before anything else, invite Christ. Do you know how to invite Him? "Whatsoever you do to the least of my brothers," He said, "you do to me."[14] Don't think that it is annoying to invite the poor for Christ's sake. Don't adorn the bride with golden ornaments, but dress her modestly. Thus from the beginning of her married life she will shun excess. Let there be no disorderly uproar. When everything is ready, call the bridegroom to receive the virgin. Let there be no drunkenness at the banquets and suppers, but an abundance of spiritual joy. Think of the many good things that will result from weddings like this! The way most weddings—if we can even call them weddings, and

---

[14]Cf Mt 25:40.

not spectacles—are celebrated nowadays ends in nothing
but evil. As soon as the banquet is over, the bride's mother
has to worry whether anything she has borrowed has been
lost or broken, and whatever pleasure she may have had is
replaced with distress when she sees what disarray her
house is in. So when Christ is present at a wedding, He
brings cheerfulness, pleasure, moderation, modesty, so-
briety, and health; but Satan brings anxiety, pain, excessive
expense, indecency, envy, and drunkenness. Let us remember all these things, and avoid such evils, that we may
please God and be counted worthy to obtain the good things
He has promised to those who love Him, through the
grace and love for mankind of our Lord Jesus Christ, with
whom, together with the Holy Spirit, be glory, honor and
power to the Father, now and ever, and unto ages of ages.
Amen.

SERMON ON MARRIAGE*

In pagan books, if anything good happens to be said, most writers hardly utter one healthful word out of many. In the holy Scriptures it is quite the reverse. There you never hear any evil word, but everything filled with salvation and great wisdom. Such are the words which have been read to us today. What are they? "Concerning the matters about which you wrote," Paul says, "it is well for a man not to touch a woman. But because of the temptation to immorality, each man should have his own wife and each woman her own husband."[1] Paul legislates concerning marriage without being ashamed or blushing, and with good reason. His Master honored a marriage, and so far from being ashamed of it, adorned the occasion with His presence and His gift. Indeed, He brought a greater wedding gift than any other, when He changed the nature of water into wine. How then could His servant blush to legislate concerning marriage?

Marriage is not an evil thing. It is adultery that is evil, it is fornication that is evil. Marriage is a remedy to eliminate fornication. Let us not, therefore, dishonor marriage by the pomp of the devil. Instead, let those who take wives now do as they did at Cana in Galilee. Let them have Christ in their midst. "How can they do this?" someone asks. By inviting the clergy. "He who receives you," the

---

*St John introduces his sermon with some advice on speaking good words and avoiding evil speech.

[1] 1 Cor 7:1-2.

Lord says, "receives Me."[2] So drive away the devil. Throw out the lewd songs, the corrupt melodies, the disorderly dances, the shameful words, the diabolical display, the uproar, the unrestrained laughter, and the rest of the impropriety. Bring in instead the holy servants of Christ, and through them Christ will certainly be present along with His mother and His brothers. For He says, "Whoever does the will of My Father is My brother and sister and mother."[3]

I know that some people think I am burdensome and difficult, giving advice like this and uprooting ancient custom. But I do not care at all about their objections. I do not seek your favor but your benefit. I do not ask for the applause of praise, but the profit of wisdom. Let no one tell me that this is the custom. Where sin is boldly committed, forget about custom. If evil things are done, even if the custom is ancient, abolish them. If they are not evil, even if they are not customary, introduce them and establish them. Actually it was not an ancient custom to celebrate weddings in a disgraceful way, but some kind of innovation. Consider how Isaac married Rebecca, how Jacob married Rachel. Scripture tells us of these weddings, and how these brides entered the households of their bridegrooms. Nothing is said about such customs. They gave banquets and dinners more lavish than usual, and invited their relatives to the weddings. Flutes, pipes, cymbals, drunken cavorting, and all the rest of our impropriety were avoided. Nowadays on the day of a wedding people dance and sing hymns to Aphrodite, songs full of adultery, corruption of marriages, illicit loves, unlawful unions, and many other impious and shameful themes. They accompany the bride in public with unseemly drunkenness and shameful speeches. How can you expect chastity of her, tell me, if you accustom her to such shamelessness from the first day,

---

[2]Mt 10:40.
[3]Mt 12:50.

if you present in her sight such actions and words as even the more serious slaves should not hear? For such a long time her father has striven along with her mother to protect the virgin, to keep her from speaking or hearing any of these words. He has arranged for private chambers, women's apartments, guards, doors, and locks. He has allowed her to go out only in the evening, to be seen only by members of the family. Have you overthrown all these precautions in one day, teaching her shamelessness by that disgraceful retinue, and introducing corrupt thoughts into the soul of the bride? Do not the subsequent evils begin here? Is not this the beginning of childlessness and widowhood and untimely orphanhood?

When you invoke demons by your songs, when you fulfill their desires by your shameful speeches, when you bring mimes and effeminate actors and the whole theater into your house, when you fill your house with harlots and arrange for the whole chorus of demons to make merry there, what good can you expect, tell me? Why do you even invite the clergy, if you are planning to celebrate these rites on the next day? Do you wish to demonstrate a beneficial munificence? Invite the choirs of the poor. Are you ashamed at this idea? Do you blush? What could be more unreasonable than this? When you drag the devil into your house, you do not think that you are doing anything shameful, but when you plan to bring Christ in, you blush? Just as Christ is present when the poor enter, so when effeminates and mimes dance there, the devil is carousing in their midst. From this extravagance there is no benefit, but rather great harm. From the other expenditure you might quickly receive a great reward.

No one in the city has done this, you say? Why don't you hurry to be the founder of this good custom, so that posterity may attribute it to you? If anyone envies or imitates this custom, your descendants will be able to say to inquirers that you first introduced this practice. In the

competitions of the unbelievers, at symposia, many people
sing the praises of those who have improved these unedi-
fying rites. All the more in the spiritual rite everyone will
give praise and thanks to the one who first introduces this
wonderful innovation. This will bring both honor and benefit to him. When this is tended by others, it will bring the
reward of its fruits to you who first planted it. This will
make you quickly a father, this will help your children
prosper, this will aid the bridegroom to grow old together
with his bride. Just as God continually threatens the sinners, saying, "Your children shall be orphans and your
wives widows,"[4] so also He promises to those who are
always obedient a pleasant old age together with every good
gift.

We can also hear Paul saying this, that a multitude of
sins often causes untimely deaths. "That is why," he says,
"many of you are weak and ill, and some have died."[5]
From the story of the girl in Joppa we can learn that the
poor who have been fed do not allow anything like this
to happen. If any misfortune occurs, they bring a quick
restoration. When she was lying dead, the poor whom she
had fed stood around weeping. They raised her up and
restored her to life.[6] So much more beneficial is the prayer
of the widows and the poor than any amount of laughter
and dancing. The latter gives pleasure for one day; the
former brings lasting benefit. Think how good it is for a
bride to enter the house of her bridegroom with such
blessings on her head. Are not these more noble than any
crowns? Are not they more useful than any wealth? Whereas the present customs represent the greatest madness and
insanity.

*   *   *

---

[4] Ex 22:24.
[5] 1 Cor 11:30.
[6] Acts 9:36-41.

Marriage was not instituted for wantonness or fornication, but for chastity. Listen to what Paul says: "Because of the temptation to immorality, each man should have his own wife and each woman her own husband."[7] These are the two purposes for which marriage was instituted: to make us chaste, and to make us parents. Of these two, the reason of chastity takes precedence. When desire began, then marriage also began. It sets a limit to desire by teaching us to keep to one wife. Marriage does not always lead to child-bearing, although there is the word of God which says, "Be fruitful and multiply, and fill the earth."[8] We have as witnesses all those who are married but childless. So the purpose of chastity takes precedence, especially now, when the whole world is filled with our kind. At the beginning, the procreation of children was desirable, so that each person might leave a memorial of his life. Since there was not yet any hope of resurrection, but death held sway, and those who died thought that they would perish after this life, God gave the comfort of children, so as to leave living images of the departed and to preserve our species. For those who were about to die and for their relatives, the greatest consolation was their offspring. To understand that this was the chief reason for desiring children, listen to the complaint of Job's wife. "See," she says, "your memory has perished from the earth, your sons and your daughters."[9] Likewise Saul says to David, "Swear to me that you will not destroy my seed, and my name along with me."[10] But now that resurrection is at our gates, and we do not speak of death, but advance toward another life better than the present, the desire for posterity is superfluous. If you desire children, you can get much better

---

[7] 1 Cor 7:2.
[8] Gen 1:28.
[9] Cf Job 18:17.
[10] 1 Kings 24:22 (1 Sam 24:21).

children now, a nobler childbirth and better help in your old age, if you give birth by spiritual labor.

So there remains only one reason for marriage, to avoid fornication, and the remedy is offered for this purpose. If you are going to practice fornication after marriage, you have approached marriage uselessly and in vain; or rather not merely in vain, but to your harm. It is not as serious for an unmarried man to practice fornication as to do the same after marriage. For then the same act is no longer fornication but adultery. Even if this statement seems strange, it is true. I realize that many people think it is adultery only when one corrupts a married woman. But I say that if a married man treats wickedly and wantonly an unmarried woman, even a prostitute or a servant girl, this act is adultery. The charge of adultery is determined not only by the status of the person wronged but also by that of the wrongdoer.

Do not tell me about the laws of the unbelievers, which drag the woman caught in adultery into court and exact a penalty, but do not demand a penalty from the married men who have corrupted servant girls. I will read to you the law of God, which is equally severe with the woman and the man, and which calls the deed adultery. When Paul says, "Let each woman have her own husband," he adds, "Let the husband show his wife the good will which is due."[11] What does he mean when he says this? Is it to preserve her access to her money? Is it to keep her dowry intact? Is it to provide her with expensive clothes, or an extravagant table, or a conspicuous display when she goes out? Is it to have her attended by many servants? What do you say? What kind of good will do you seek? All of these things show good will, do they not? I do not mean any of these, Paul says, but chastity and holiness. The husband's body is no longer the husband's, but the wife's. Therefore

---

[11] 1 Cor 7:2-3 var.

he must keep her property intact, without diminishing it or damaging it. We say that that servant has good will who takes charge of his master's property and does not damage any of it. Since therefore the husband's body is the wife's property, the husband must show good will in regard to the property entrusted to him. When Paul says, "Let him show the good will which is due," he adds, "the wife does not rule over her own body, but the husband does; likewise the husband does not rule over his own body, but the wife does."[12] So when you see a prostitute setting snares, plotting against you, desiring your body, say to her, "This body is not mine. It belongs to my wife. I do not dare to mistreat it nor to lend it to another woman." The wife should do the same. Here there is complete equality.

I grant that in other matters Paul gives the husband superior authority, when he says, "Let each one of you love his wife as himself, and let the wife see that she respects her husband."[13] He also says, "The husband is the head of the wife," and, "The wife ought to be subject to her husband."[14] In the Old Testament it is written, "Your desire shall be for your husband, and he shall rule over you."[15] How then in this passage has Paul introduced an equal exchange of service and mastery? In saying, "The wife does not rule over her own body, but the husband does; likewise the husband does not rule over his own body, but the wife does,"[16] he introduces a great measure of equality. Just as the husband is master of her body, so the wife is mistress of his body. Why does Paul introduce so much equality? Although in other matters there needs to be a superior authority, here where chastity and holiness are at

---

[12]1 Cor 7:3-4.
[13]Eph 5:33.
[14]Eph 5:23, 24.
[15]Gen 3:16.
[16]1 Cor 7:4.

stake, the husband has no greater privilege than the wife. He is punished equally with her if he breaks the laws of marriage, and with good reason. Your wife did not come to you, leaving her father and mother and her whole household, so that you could dishonor her, so that you could take a cheap servant girl in her place. It was not in order to start a thousand battles that you took a companion, a partner for your life, a free woman of equal honor with yourself. Would it not be foolish to receive her dowry, treat it with all good will, and diminish nothing of it, but to corrupt and ruin that which is more valuable than the whole dowry, namely chastity and holiness, as well as your own body which is her possession? If you diminish her dowry, you give cause for a lawsuit to your father-in-law. If you diminish chastity, you will pay the penalty to God who instituted marriage and protects the wife. To know that this is true, hear what Paul says about adulterers: "Whoever disregards this, disregards not man but God, who gives His Holy Spirit to you."[17] Do you see how definitely his words prove that it is adultery to corrupt not only a married woman but even a prostitute, if the man is married? Just as we say that a married woman is made an adultress whether she sins with a servant or any other man, so we should say that a married man commits adultery if he sins with a servant girl or any loose woman. Therefore do not neglect your own salvation. Do not offer your soul to the devil by this kind of sin. By such sins many families are broken, many battles are started. Such sins empty out love and undermine good will. Just as a virtuous man can never neglect or scorn his wife, so a wanton and licentious man can never love his wife, no matter how beautiful she is. Virtue gives birth to love, and love brings innumerable blessings.

(St John continues to exhort the husband to fidelity.)

---

[17] 1 Thess 4:8.

HOW TO CHOOSE A WIFE*

Today I shall speak about the same subject. I wish to give advice to those who want to enter marriage. When we are about to buy households and slaves, we are very curious and nosy about the sellers and the previous owners, and about the individuals we are buying. We want to know the condition of their bodies and the disposition of their souls. When we are about to marry a wife, we ought to show even more foresight. If a house is defective we can return it, and if a slave is clumsy we can take him back to the seller. When we take a wife we cannot return her to her family, but we must keep her with us until the end. If we reject her because she is bad, we are guilty of adultery according to the law of God. So when you are going to take a wife, do not read the laws of the state only, but first of all read the laws of the Church. God will judge you at the last day not by the civil law but by His law. Neglect of the civil law often brings fines in money. Neglect of God's law brings inescapable punishment for the soul and that unquenchable fire.

When you are about to take a wife, you rush eagerly to the experts in civil law. You sit beside them and question them carefully. "What will happen if my wife dies childless? What if she has a child, or two or three? How will she be able to use her money if her father is living, or if he is not? What part of the inheritance will go to her

---

*St John begins with praise of the previous preacher, probably Bishop Maximos, and reference to his own sermon on marriage and adultery.

brothers and sisters, what part to her husband? When will her husband gain control of the whole, without allowing anyone to detach any part of her property? Under what conditions will he be deprived of the whole?" You ask many other questions like these with great curiosity, investigating everything to make sure that no part of your wife's property goes to any of her relatives. As I said before, if anything unexpected should happen the penalty would be only money; nevertheless you are not willing to overlook any of these possibilities. Isn't this foolish? When we are in danger of losing money we take so much care, but when we are risking our souls and the punishment hereafter, we pay no attention. We ought to be concerned and take trouble about these matters above all.

I advise, therefore, and exhort those who are about to marry that they should approach the blessed Paul and read the laws which he has recorded concerning marriage. First learn what he bids you to do if your wife happens to be wicked, deceitful, alcoholic, abusive, foolish, or subject to any other such fault. Then discuss marriage with this in mind. If you see that he allows you to divorce her and take another if you find any of these faults in her, then enjoy your freedom from care. If, however, he does not allow this, but bids you to be content and keep her with you in spite of any fault except unchastity, then make your resolve firm to endure all your wife's wickedness. If this is heavy and burdensome, then take every care to choose a good, kind, docile wife. You know that you must make one of two choices. If you take a bad wife, you must endure the annoyance. If you are not willing to do this, you incur the guilt of adultery by divorcing her. The Lord says, "Everyone who divorces his wife, except on the ground of unchastity, makes her an adulteress; and whoever marries a divorced woman commits adultery."[1] If we have investi-

---

[1]Mt 5:32.

gated these laws and know them well before we marry, we will take great care to choose a wife who is well-ordered from the beginning and compatible with our character. If we marry a woman like this, we will gain not only the benefit that we will never divorce her, but also that we will love her intensely, as Paul commands. For when he says, "Husbands, love your wives," he does not stop with this, but gives us a measure for love, "as Christ loved the Church."² And how did Christ love the Church? Tell me. "He gave Himself up for her." So even if you must die for your wife, do not refuse. If the Master loved His servant so much that He gave Himself up for her, all the more you must love your fellow servant as much.

Let us see, however, whether perhaps the beauty of the bride attracted the Bridegroom, and the virtue of her soul. No: she was unattractive and impure, as the next words show. When Paul says, "He gave Himself up for her," he adds, "that He might sanctify her, having cleansed her by the washing of water."³ When he says, "having cleansed her," he shows that she was unclean and unholy—not in any ordinary way, but with the greatest uncleanness. She was defiled with grease, smoke, blood, gore, and innumerable stains like these.⁴ Nevertheless He did not abhor her ugliness, but changed her repulsiveness, reshaped her, reformed her, remitted her sins. You must imitate Him. Even if your wife sins against you more times than you can count, you must forgive and pardon everything. If you marry a surly woman, you must reform her with gentleness and kindness, as Christ did the Church. He did not only wipe away her uncleanness but even stripped off her old age, taking off the old humanity which is composed of sin. Paul hints at this also: "That He might present the Church

---

²Eph 5:25.
³Eph 5:26.
⁴These stains suggest animal sacrifice, whether Jewish or pagan.

to Himself in splendor, without spot or wrinkle."[5] He did not make her merely beautiful but also young, not according to the nature of her body, but according to the state of her character. And this is not the only marvel, that when He found her ugly, shameful, and old He did not abhor her ugliness but handed Himself over to death and refashioned her in unimaginable beauty. It is even more marvelous that after this, when He often sees her soiled and spotted, He does not reject her nor cast her away from Himself, but continues to care for her and correct her. How many, tell me, have sinned after coming to the Faith? Yet He did not abhor them. For example, the immoral man at Corinth was a member of the Church; He did not cut off the member, but cured it.[6] The whole church of the Galatians was rebellious, and fell into Judaizing practices; yet He did not cast them out either, but took care of them by Paul's agency and restored them to their former relationship. When there is an infection in our bodies, we do not cut off the limb, but try to expel the disease. We must do the same with a wife. If there is some wickedness in her, do not reject your wife, but expel the evil. After all, it is possible for a wife to reform, but it is often impossible for an injured limb to recover. Yet even when we know that the injury is incurable, we still do not cut off the limb. Often a person with a crooked foot, a lame leg, a dry and withered hand, or a sightless eye does not put out the eye or cut off the leg or the hand. Instead, even though he sees that no benefit comes to the body from the diseased part, and indeed much shame comes upon the other limbs, he goes on keeping it because of its affinity with the rest. Isn't this foolish? When the cure is impossible and there is no benefit, we exercise such care; but when there is good hope of amendment, we refuse the treatment. When some-

---

[5]Eph 5:27.
[6]1 Cor 5.

thing is injured in its nature it cannot recover, but the crooked inclination can be reformed.

Even if you should say that your wife is incurably ill, and after receiving much care still behaves in her own manner, still you must not cast her out. The limb with an incurable disease is not cut off. She also is your limb, for it is written, "The two shall become one flesh."[7] Besides, with the limb, we receive no benefit from the treatment when the illness turns out to be incurable; but with a wife, even if she remains incurably ill, we will receive a great reward for our attempts to teach and educate her. Even if she does not benefit at all from our teaching, we will receive a great reward from God for our patience, because we have shown so much forbearance through fear of Him. We have endured her evil ways with gentleness and have kept our member. For a wife is a member which is related to us, and because of this we especially ought to love her. This is just what Paul was teaching when he said, "Even so husbands should love their wives as their own bodies . . . For no man ever hates his own flesh, but nourishes and cherishes it, as Christ does the Church, because we are members of His body, made from His flesh and His bones."[8] Just as Eve came from the side of Adam, he says, so we come from the side of Christ.[9] This is what he means when he says, "made from His flesh and His bones." We all know that Eve came from the side of Adam himself. Scripture has told this plainly, that God put Adam into a deep sleep and took one of his ribs, and fashioned the woman. But how can we show that the Church also came from the side of Christ? Scripture explains this too. When Christ was lifted up on the cross, after He had been nailed to it and had died, one of the soldiers pierced His side and there

---

[7]Gen 2:24, Mt 19:5, Eph 5:31.
[8]Eph 5:28-30 (variant reading).
[9]The same word πλευρά is used for "rib" and "side."

came out blood and water.[10] From that blood and water
the whole Church has arisen. He Himself bears witness to
this when He says, "Unless one is born again of water and
spirit, he cannot enter the kingdom of heaven."[11] He calls
the blood "spirit." We receive birth from the water of
baptism, and we are nourished by His blood. Do you see
how we are made from His flesh and from His bones, as
we are given birth and nourished by that blood and water?
Just as the woman was fashioned while Adam slept, so
also, when Christ had died, the Church was formed from
His side.

We must love our wife not only because she is a part
of ourselves and had the beginning of her creation from us,
but also because God made a law about this when He
said, "For this reason a man shall leave his father and his
mother, and shall cleave to his wife, and the two shall become one flesh."[12] Paul reads us this law in order to surround us and drive us toward this love. See the wisdom
of the apostle. He does not lead us to the love of our
wives by divine laws only, or by human reasoning only,
but by interchanging them he makes a combination of both.
In this way the wiser and higher-minded may be led by the
heavenly arguments, while the weaker may be led to love
by the natural and earthly arguments. This is why he begins with Christ's righteous acts, and introduces his exhortation by saying, "Love your wives as Christ loved the
Church." Then again from human experience: "Husbands
ought to love their wives as their own bodies." Then again
from Christ: "Because we are members of His body, made
from His flesh and His bones." Then again from humanity:
"For this reason a man shall leave his father and his
mother, and shall cleave to his wife."

---

[10]John 19:34.
[11]John 3:5 (variant reading).
[12]Gen 2:24, Eph 5:31.

After reading this law, Paul says, "This is a great mystery."[13] How is it a great mystery? Tell me. Because the girl who has always been kept at home and has never seen the bridegroom, from the first day loves and cherishes him as her own body. Again, the husband, who has never seen her, never shared even the fellowship of speech with her, from the first day prefers her to everyone, to his friends, his relatives, even his parents. The parents in turn, if they are deprived of their money for another reason, will complain, grieve, and take the perpetrators to court. Yet they entrust to a man, whom often they have never seen before or come to know at all, both their own daughter and a large sum as dowry. They rejoice as they do this and do not consider it a loss. As they see their daughter led away, they do not bring to mind their closeness, they do not grieve or complain, but instead they give thanks. They consider it an answer to their prayers when they see their daughter led away from their home taking a large sum of money with her. Paul had all this in mind: how the couple leave their parents and bind themselves to each other, and how the new relationship becomes more powerful than the long-established familiarity. He saw that this was not a human accomplishment. It is God who sows these loves in men and women. He causes both those who give in marriage and those who are married to do this with joy. Therefore Paul said, "This is a great mystery."

Just as in the case of children, the baby which is born immediately from the first sight recognizes its parents without being able to speak, so also the hearts of the bride and bridegroom are entwined together at the first sight without anyone to introduce them, to advise them, or to counsel them. Then, seeing that this happened also above all with Christ and the Church, Paul was astonished and amazed. How did this happen with Christ and the Church?

---

[13]Eph 5:32.

As the bridegroom leaves his father and comes to his bride, so Christ left His Father's throne and came to His bride. He did not summon us on high, but Himself came to us (of course when you hear that He left, you must not imagine a change but a condescension; for even when He was with us, He was still with the Father). For this reason when Paul said, "This is a great mystery," he added, "I understand it in relation to Christ and the Church."[14] Since you know, therefore, how great a mystery marriage is, and how great a matter it represents, do not consider marriage lightly or casually.

In particular, you must not seek money when you are about to take a bride. You must consider that marriage is not a business venture but a fellowship for life. I hear many of you saying, "So and so got rich from his marriage, although he was poor before. Since he took a rich wife, he enjoys wealth and luxury now." What are you saying, man? Do you desire to profit from your wife? Aren't you ashamed? Don't you blush? Why don't you sink into the ground, if you seek to benefit yourself in such a way? What kind of words are these for a husband? A wife has only one duty, to preserve what we have gathered, to protect our income, to take care of our household. After all, God gave her to us for this purpose, to help us in these matters as well as in everything else. In general our life is composed of two spheres of activity, the public and the private. When God divided these two He assigned the management of the household to the woman, but to the men He assigned all the affairs of the city, all the business of the marketplace, courts, council-chambers, armies, and all the rest. A woman cannot throw a spear or hurl a javelin, but she can take up the distaff, weave cloth, and manage everything else well that concerns the household. She cannot give an opinion in the council, but she can give

---

[14]Eph 5:32.

her opinion in the household. Often, indeed, whatever her husband knows of household matters, she knows better. She cannot manage the affairs of the city well, but she can raise children well, which are the greatest of treasures. She can discover the misbehavior of the maids and oversee the virtue of the servants. She can free her husband from all cares and worries for the house, the store-rooms, the wool-working, the preparation of meals, the maintenance of clothing. She takes care of all the other matters which it is not fitting or easy for a man to undertake no matter how competitive he might be. After all, this is the work of God's generosity and wisdom, that he who is good at the greater matters is inferior and quite useless in the lesser matters, so that the help of a woman is necessary to him. If God had made man capable in both areas, it would have been easy for men to despise womankind. If, on the other hand, God had assigned the greater and more important matters to woman, He would have filled women with presumption. For this reason He did not give both spheres to one sex, lest the other seem inferior and superfluous. Neither did He assign both spheres to each sex equally, lest from equality of honor there should arise strife and contention, if women strove to be counted worthy of the same precedence as their husbands. God provided for peace by reserving the suitable position for each. He divided our life into these two parts, and gave the more necessary and important to the man, but the lesser and inferior part to the woman. In this way He arranged that we should admire the man more because we need his service more, and that because the woman has a humbler form of service she would not rebel against her husband.

Since we know all this, let us seek just one thing in a wife, virtue of soul and nobility of character, so that we may enjoy tranquillity, so that we may luxuriate in harmony and lasting love. The man who takes a rich wife takes a boss rather than a wife. If even without wealth women are

filled with pride and prone to the love of fame, if they have
wealth in addition, how will their husbands be able to stand
them? The man, however, who takes a wife of equal position or poorer than himself takes a helper and ally, and
brings every blessing into his house. Her own poverty
forces her to care for her husband with great concern, to
yield to him and obey him in everything. It removes every
occasion for strife, battle, presumption, and pride. It binds
the couple in peace, harmony, love, and concord. Let us
not, therefore, seek to have money, but to have peace, in
order to enjoy happiness. Marriage does not exist to fill
our houses with war and battles, to give us strife and contention, to pit us against each other and make our life
unlivable. It exists in order that we may enjoy another's
help, that we may have a harbor, a refuge, and a consolation in the troubles which hang over us, and that we may
converse happily with our wife. How many wealthy men
who have taken rich wives and increased their substance
have yet destroyed their happiness and harmony, as they
contend in daily battles at table? How many poor men
who have taken poorer wives now enjoy peace and look
upon each day's sun with joy? Rich men, although they
are surrounded by luxury, have often on account of their
wives prayed to die and be relieved of the present life.
Thus money is of no use when we do not have a partner
with a good soul.

Besides, why should I speak of peace and harmony?
Even in the acquisition of money we are often hindered
by taking a rich wife. When a man has reckoned all his
profits to the account of the dowry, if an untimely death
occurs, he is forced to pay the whole amount to his
in-laws. Like someone who has suffered shipwreck on the
sea and saved only his body, so this man comes forth from
a storm of contention, strife, insolent acts, and law-suits
only just keeping his body free. Just as insatiable merchants, by filling their ship with uncountable wares and

loading it with an excessive burden, have often sunk their vessel and lost everything, so these men have incurred over-burdensome marriages, thinking that they will collect a greater substance through their wives, and have lost even what they had. Just as on the sea the sudden shock of a wave falls on the vessel and sinks it, so here an untimely death falls upon him and takes away along with his wife all his possessions.

Since we know all this, let us not investigate our bride's money, but the gentleness of her character and her piety and chastity. A wife who is chaste, gentle, and moderate, even if she is poor, can make poverty better than wealth. Likewise a wife who is corrupt, undisciplined, and contentious, even if she has immeasurable treasure stored away, blows it away more quickly than any wind and surrounds her husband with innumerable misfortunes along with poverty. So let us not seek a wealthy wife, but one who will use well what we have.

You must learn first what the purpose of marriage is, and why it was introduced into our life. Do not ask anything else. What then is the reason for marriage, and why did God give it to us? Listen to what Paul says: "Because of the temptation to immorality let each man have his own wife."[15] He does not say, "Because of the relief from poverty," or "Because of the acquisition of wealth," but what? In order that we may avoid fornication, restrain our desire, practice chastity, and be well pleasing to God by being satisfied with our own wife: this is the gift of marriage, this is its fruit, this is its profit. Do not, therefore, neglect the greater benefit and seek the lesser. Wealth is far inferior to chastity. We should seek a wife for this reason only, in order to avoid sin, to be freed from all immorality. To this end every marriage should be set up so that it may work together with us for chastity. This will

---

[15] 1 Cor 7:2.

be the case if we marry such brides as are able to bring great piety, chastity, and goodness to us. The beauty of the body, if it is not joined with virtue of the soul, will be able to hold a husband for twenty or thirty days, but will go no farther before it shows its wickedness and destroys all its attractiveness. As for those who radiate the beauty of the soul, the longer time goes by and tests their proper nobility, the warmer they make their husband's love and the more they strengthen their affection for him. Since this is so, and since a warm and genuine friendship holds between them, every kind of immorality is driven out. Not even any thought of wantonness ever enters the mind of the man who truly loves his own wife, but he continues always content with her. By his chastity he attracts the good will and protection of God for his whole household. This is how the good men of ancient times used to take wives, seeking nobility of soul rather than monetary wealth.

As evidence that what I say is true, I will mention one marriage in particular. "Now Abraham was old and well advanced in years," the Scripture says. "He said to his servant, the oldest of his house, who had charge of all that he had, 'Put your hand under my thigh, and I will make you swear by the Lord, the God of heaven and earth, that you will not take a wife for my son Isaac from the daughters of the Canaanites, among whom I dwell, but will go to my country and to my kindred, and take a wife for my son from there.' "[16] Do you see the virtue of the righteous man? Do you see how much foresight he used in regard to the marriage? He did not summon a procuress, as people do now, or a matchmaker, or any drunken old woman. He entrusted the matter to his own servant. In itself this is great evidence of the patriarch's discretion, that he had trained a servant so well that he could be considered a trustworthy agent in so great a matter. Then, you see, he

---

[16]Gen 24:1-4.

did not seek a rich or beautiful wife, but one who would be noble in her character. This is why he sent his servant so far away from home. Notice also the loyalty of the servant. He did not say, "What is this? There are so many tribes near us, so many daughters of rich men, notable and distinguished men, but you are sending me to such a distant country, to unknown people. With whom shall I speak? Who will know me? What if they set a trap for me, if they try to deceive me? It is not easy to undertake anything like this when you are a stranger." He did not say any of these things, but passing over all of them, he was anxious about the one thing which merited anxiety. By not making any objection, he showed his obedience. By asking only that which he most needed to inquire, he revealed his intelligence and foresight. So what was this one thing? What did he ask his master? "If the woman is not willing to come with me, shall I take your son back to the land from which you came?" Then Abraham said, "Do not take my son back there: The Lord, the God of heaven and earth, who took me from my father's house and from the land of my birth, and who spoke to me and swore to me, 'To your descendents I will give this land,' He will send His angel before you and make your journey prosperous."[17] Do you see the man's faith? He did not summon friends or relatives or anyone else, but gave him God as a go-between and traveling companion. Then, wishing to encourage his servant, he did not simply say, "The Lord, the God of heaven and earth," but he added, "who took me from my father's house." It is as if he said, "Remember what a long way we traveled, how we left our own prosperity and came to enjoy greater prosperity in a strange land, how the impossible became possible." It was not only to explain this that he said, "Who took me from my father's house,"

---

[17]Gen 24:5-7.

but also to show that God owed him something. "He is
in debt to us," Abraham says; "He Himself said, 'I will
give this land to you and to your seed.'"[18] So even if we are
unworthy, yet because of His promise, in order to bring
it to fulfillment, He will be with us, He will make all our
tasks easy, and He will accomplish this undertaking for
which we pray." With these words he sent the servant on
his way.

Then, when the servant arrived in that country, he did
not approach anyone who lived in the city. He did not
speak with people or ask to see any women. See how
faithful he was. He kept to the go-between whom he had
accepted. He spoke only with Him. He stood and prayed,
and he said, "O Lord, God of my master Abraham, grant
me success today."[19] He did not say, "O Lord my God,"
but what? "O Lord, God of my master Abraham." He
means, "Even if I am worthless rubbish, I bring my master
forward. I do not come for my own purpose but in his
service. Respecting his virtue, therefore, I pray Thee to
accomplish all my undertaking." Then, lest you think that
he asks as if for a debt, listen to what follows: "Show
mercy to my master Abraham." He means, "Even if we
have done many righteous deeds, we ask to be saved by
grace. We ask to receive our request from Thy love and
not as a debt or an obligation." So what does he want?
"Behold, I am standing by the spring of water, and the
daughters of the inhabitants of the city are coming out to
draw water. Let the maiden to whom I shall say, 'Pray let
down your jar that I may drink,' and who shall say, 'Drink,
and I will water your camels, until they all have done
drinking'—let her be the one whom Thou hast appointed
for Thy servant Isaac. By this I shall know that Thou hast

---

[18]Gen 13:15.
[19]Gen 24:12.

shown mercy to my master Abraham."[20] We can see the servant's wisdom in his choice of a sign. He did not say, "If I see a girl riding in a carriage drawn by mules, followed by a crowd of eunuchs and servants, comely and resplendent with bodily beauty, let this be the one whom Thou hast appointed for Thy servant." What did he say? "The one to whom I shall say, 'Let down your jar that I may drink.' " What are you doing, man? Are you looking for such a lowly wife for your master, one who carries her own water, and who is allowed to speak with you, a strange man? "Yes," he says, "for he did not send me to look for monetary wealth or high birth but nobility of soul. Often many of these women who carry water have a full inheritance of virtue, while others who sit around in fancy houses are more common and worse than anyone." Then how will you know that the woman is virtuous? "From the sign," he says, "which I named." How is this a sign of virtue? "It is a most unmistakable sign. This is a great enough sign of generosity to provide full proof." What he says is indeed such a sign, even if he does not utter these words: "I am looking for the kind of girl who is so hospitable that she will offer all the service in her power." He has a special reason for seeking a generous girl. Since he came from a household in which the deeds of hospitality especially flourished, he sought above all to choose a woman whose character would be compatible with his masters'. "We are going to bring her," he says, "into a household which is open to strangers. I wish to forestall the war and strife which might occur if the husband gives away their substance freely after his father's example and welcomes strangers, while the wife stingily objects and tries to prevent it, as happens in many households. To avoid such a situation, I want to know at once whether she is hospitable. Everything good which has happened to us came because

---

[20]Gen 24:13-14.

of hospitality. Because of this my master obtained the bridegroom: because of this he became a father. He killed the calf and received a child, mixed wheat-meal and received God's promise to give him offspring as many as the stars.[21] So since everything good which has happened to us and our household came because of hospitality, this is what I seek above all." Let us not see only the fact that he asked for water, but let us consider that it shows a truly generous soul not only to give what is asked but to provide more than what is requested.

"And it came to pass," the Scripture says, "before he had done speaking, behold Rebecca came out;"[22] and the word of the prophet was fulfilled, "While you are still speaking, I will say, 'Behold I am here.' "[23] Such are the prayers of truly noble men. Before they finish they persuade God to accede to their words. You too, therefore, when you are going to take a wife, do not seek human aid, nor have recourse to women who trade in others' misfortunes and whose only object is to obtain a profit for themselves. Turn to God for help. He is not ashamed to become your matchmaker. He Himself promised this when He said, "Seek the kingdom of heaven, and all this shall be added to you."[24] Do not say, "How can I see God? He will not speak to me with a voice and converse openly, will He, so that I may go and ask Him?" These are the words of a soul with little faith. God can quickly arrange everything He wishes even without using a voice. Indeed this is what happened in this case. The servant did not hear a voice or see any vision. As he stood at the spring, he prayed, and at once he obtained his request. "It came to pass," the Scripture says, "before he had done speaking, Rebecca,

---

[21]Gen 18:6-7, 22.17.
[22]Gen 24:15.
[23]Is 58:9.
[24]Mt 6:33.

who was born to Bethuel the son of Milcah, came out with
her water jar upon her shoulder. The maiden was very
fair to look upon, a virgin, whom no man had known."[25]
Why do you tell me about the beauty of her body? To
teach you the preeminence of her chastity, to teach you the
beauty of her soul. Chastity is wonderful, and it is even
more wonderful when it occurs together with physical
beauty. For this reason also when the Scripture is going to
tell us about Joseph and his chastity, it mentions first the
beauty of his body: "Joseph was handsome and good-
looking."[26] Then it tells about his chastity, showing that his
beauty did not lead him into licentiousness. For beauty
does not cause immorality, nor ugliness produce chastity
in every case. Many women who shine out with physical
beauty shine even more with their chastity. Others who are
shameful and ugly in appearance are even uglier in their
souls, stained with countless immoralities. It is not the
nature of the body but the inclination of the soul which
produces either chastity or immorality.

It is not a mere repetition when Rebecca is called a
virgin twice. When Moses says, "She was a virgin," he
adds, "whom no man had known." Many virgins keep their —
bodies uncorrupted, but fill their souls with all kinds of
licentiousness. They adorn themselves, attract innumerable
admirers, and excite the eyes of the young men, setting
ambushes and traps for them. Moses shows that Rebecca
was not that kind of girl, but was a virgin in both body
and soul: "She was a virgin, whom no man had known."
Indeed there were many reasons why she might have become known to men: first, the beauty of her body, and
second, the kind of work that she did. If she had sat all the
time in her chambers, as girls do nowadays, and had never
entered the market-place nor left her father's house, there

---

[25]Gen 24:15-16.
[26]Gen 39:6.

would not be so much reason to praise her for being unknown to men. But she went out to the market-place
because she was obliged to fetch water every day, once or
twice or many times, and yet she was not known to any
man. So you can understand why she deserves especial
praise. A girl who rarely approaches the market-place, who
is rather plain and unattractive, and is accompanied by
many servants, nevertheless often has her morals corrupted
by these excursions. This girl went out of her father's house
alone every day, and not only to the market-place but to
the spring to draw water, where she had to meet many
people of all sorts. How could we help admiring her, since
her morals were not at all corrupted by her continual er-
rands, by her lovely face, or by the crowds of people she
encountered? Instead she kept her body and soul pure, and
preserved her chastity better than those who sit at home
in the women's quarters. She was the kind of girl whom
Paul sought, the one who is "holy in body and spirit."[27]

"She went down to the spring, and filled her jar, and
came up. Then the servant ran to meet her, and said, 'Pray
give me a little water to drink from your jar.' She said,
'Drink, my lord;' and she quickly let down her jar upon
her hand, and gave him a drink. When he had finished
drinking, she said, 'I will draw for your camels also, until
all of them drink.' So she quickly emptied her jar into the
trough and ran again to the well to draw and bring water
for all his camels."[28] Great was the generosity of this
woman, and great was her modesty. You may learn both
these virtues of hers from what she did and what she said.
Do you see how her modesty did not spoil her generosity,
nor her generosity corrupt her modesty? Because of her
modesty she did not run to meet the man nor address him
first. Because of her generosity and hospitality she did not

---

[27] 1 Cor 7:34.
[28] Gen 24:16-20.

refuse or deny what he requested. If she had run up to him and addressed him before he said anything, we would call her bold and shameless. If she had avoided him when he asked for help, we would call her cruel and inhuman. In fact she did not do either of these things. She did not spoil her generosity because of her modesty, nor because of her generosity did she make herself less deserving to be praised for her modesty. She showed the full measure of each virtue. She proved her modesty by waiting for his request, and her great generosity by assisting him after his request. Indeed, it indicates great generosity not only to give what is asked but to offer even more than what is requested. If what she gave was only water, that is what she had in her power at the time. We judge generosity not by the value of the gift but by the resources of the giver. God praised the person who gave a cup of cold water.[29] He also said that the woman who contributed two small coins had given more than all the others, since she had given everything she had.[30] In the same way, Rebecca welcomed that noble stranger with the best that she could offer him.

The words "quickly" and "she ran" show you how eagerly Rebecca did the deed, not unwillingly, not as if forced, not with vexation or annoyance. We know from experience that this is not a small matter. We have often asked someone who was passing by with a torch to stop a moment and give us a light, or someone who was carrying water to give us a drink, and he has not granted it but instead has become angry. She, however, not only let down her jar for him but even drew water for all his camels. She undertook so much effort and offered her physical labor for the sake of hospitality with great politeness. Her virtue appears not only in what she did but in her willingness in

[29]Mt 10:42.
[30]Luke 21:2-4.

doing it. She even called the man "my lord" although he
was unknown to her and had just appeared for the first
time. Her father-in-law Abraham did not ask the travelers,
"Who are you? Where do you live? Where are you going?
Where have you come from?" He simply earned the credit
for hospitality. In the same way Rebecca did not say,
"Who are you? Where do you live? Why have you come
here?" She gained the credit for hospitality and omitted
everything superfluous. Those who sell pearls for gold
seek only one thing, to make a profit from the people with
money, not to investigate their backgrounds. She also
sought only this one thing, to receive the profit of hospitality, to gain the fitting reward. She knew very well that a
stranger is often ashamed to ask for what he needs. For
this reason the situation calls for great good will, and for
uninquisitive self-restraint. If we are too inquisitive and
nosy, the stranger hesitates and shrinks back, and goes un-
happily on his way. This is why she did not ask questions
of the man, nor her father-in-law of the three strangers, in
order not to flush the quarry. He just took care of the
travelers, and when he had gained from them what he
wished, he sent them on their way. So that time he even
entertained angels. If he had been inquisitive, the reward
laid up for him would have been reduced. Indeed we admire him not so much for entertaining angels as for entertaining them unawares.[31] If he had served them knowingly,
he would not have been doing anything remarkable. A
worthy guest forces even the most stony and hard-hearted
host to become loving and gentle. What is remarkable in
this case is that, thinking they were mere travelers, he took
such good care of them. Rebecca was the same kind of
person. She did not know who the man was, nor for what
purpose he had come, nor that he had come to court her.
She thought he was just some stranger and traveler. There-

[31]Heb 13:2.

fore her reward for hospitality became greater, because she welcomed a man who was completely unknown to her with so much good will, yet at the same time she preserved her modesty.

Rebecca did not act shamelessly or boldly, nor unwillingly and angrily, but with suitable dignity. Moses hinted at this when he said, "The man gazed at her in silence to learn whether the Lord had prospered his journey."[32] What does it mean, "he gazed at her"? He studied carefully how she dressed, how she walked, how she looked at him, how she spoke, and everything else, learning the condition of her soul from the movement of her body. He was not satisfied with this only, but he set a second test. When she had given him a drink, he did not stop with this, but said to her, "Tell me whose daughter you are. Is there room in your father's house for us to lodge in?"[33] So what did she do? Patiently and politely she told him her father's name, without getting annoyed or saying, "Who are you to be so nosy, to ask questions and be curious about my household?" What did she say? "I am the daughter of Bethuel the son of Milcah, whom she bore to Nahor. We have both straw and provender enough, and room to lodge in."[34] As with the water, she gave more than he asked. He asked only for water to drink, but she promised to water the camels as well; and she watered them. The same happened in this case. He asked only for a place, but she offered straw and provender and many other things. She used all this to attract him and draw him to her house, so that she might earn the reward of hospitality. Let us not just listen to this as if it were an unimportant matter. Let us consider ourselves and compare ourselves to these people. In this way we shall recognize the woman's goodness. We often

---

[32]Gen 24:21.
[33]Gen 24:23.
[34]Gen 24:24-25.

get annoyed at entertaining acquaintances and friends. If
they stay a day or two, we feel burdened. She drew a
complete stranger into her house with great eagerness. She
was prepared to offer this service not only to him but also
to so many camels.

From what he did when he entered the house, you may
see the man's wisdom. As they gave him bread to eat, he
said, "I will not eat until I have told my errand."[35] Do you
see how vigilant and sober he was? Then, when they bade
him speak, let us see how he conversed with them. Did
he speak words like these, telling them that his master was
well-known and illustrious, honored by everyone, enjoying
precedence among the people of his country? Indeed, if he
had wished to say this, he would not have been at a loss
for words. After all, Abraham's neighbors honored him
like a king. Nevertheless he did not say any of these
things. He passed over these human concerns and praised
his master for what came from above, saying, "I am
Abraham's servant. The Lord has greatly blessed my master,
and he has become great. He has given him flocks and
herds, gold and silver."[36] He mentioned the wealth not to
show that Abraham was rich, but to show that he loved
God. He wished to praise his master not for having obtained
wealth but for having received it from God. Then he spoke
about the bridegroom: "Sarah, my master's wife, bore one
son to my master when he was old."[37] Here he hinted at
the character of the pregnancy, showing that the birth came
about by God's providence towards Abraham, not by the
course of nature. You too, you see, when you are looking
for a bridegroom or a bride, ask this first of all, whether
your intended is loved by God and enjoys good will from
above. If these blessings are present, everything else fol-

---

[35]Gen 24:33.
[36]Gen 24:34-35.
[37]Gen 24:36.

lows. If they are absent, even if the goods of this life are present in great abundance, they are of no benefit. Then, to keep his hosts from saying, "Why did he not marry any of the women of his country?" the servant said, "My master made me swear, saying, 'You shall not take a wife for my son from the daughter of the Canaanites, but you shall go to my father's house and to my kindred, and take a wife for my son.' "[38] However, not to bore you by telling the whole story, let us go to the end. When he had told how he stood at the spring, how he asked the girl, how she gave him more than he asked, and how God became the match-maker, he stopped speaking. When they heard all of this, they were no longer doubtful or hesitant. As if God were moving their souls to this purpose, they immediately promised their daughter to him. Laban and Bethuel answered, "The command has come from the Lord. We cannot give you a negative answer. Behold, here is Rebecca. Take her and go, and she shall be the wife of your master, as the Lord has spoken."[39] Who would not be amazed? Who would not marvel, seeing how many obstacles were removed in a moment of time? He was a stranger, a servant, and unknown to them. He had come a long distance. Neither the father-in-law nor the bridegroom nor any of his relatives was known to them. Any one of these facts would have been enough to prevent the marriage. Yet nothing prevented it. Everything became easy. They cheerfully entrusted the bride to him as if he were a well-known neighbor and had associated with them from his earliest days. This happened because God was in their midst. If we try to do something without Him, even if it all seems smooth and easy, we find crevasses, cliffs, and innumerable setbacks in our way. Conversely, if God is present and assisting us, even if the undertaking is the most difficult of all, everything becomes

---

[38]Gen 24:37-38.
[39]Gen 24:50-51.

smooth and easy. Let us therefore neither do nor say anything before we call upon God and beseech Him to assist with everything which we have in hand, just as Abraham's servant did.

Now let us see, once he had obtained the bride, how he arranged the wedding celebration. Did he bring along a load of cymbals, pipes, drums, flutes, singers, dancers, and all that kind of display? None of these, but taking Rebecca alone he departed. To escort and accompany her he had with him the same angel whom his master had besought God to send along with him when he set out from his house. For the rest, the bride was wedded without hearing flutes, lyres, or any other instruments, but bearing innumerable blessings from God on her head, a crown more glorious than any diadem. She was wedded wearing no golden robe but chastity, piety, generosity, and every other virtue. She was wedded not riding in an enclosed carriage or any such ostentatious vehicle, but sitting on her camel. Along with virtue in their souls, the maidens of ancient times used to have a great vigor in their bodies. Their mothers did not raise them as mothers do now, corrupting them with frequent baths, perfumed ointments, cosmetics, soft garments, and many other such influences, making them weaker than they should be. Those mothers gave their daughters all kinds of hardy training. Because of this the beauty of their bodies had a genuine freshness, as it was natural and not artificial or deliberately cultivated. For this reason they enjoyed pure good health. They had extraordinary beauty, since no weakness troubled their bodies and all indolence was banished from them. Toil, hardship, and doing all their own work drove out all frivolity and made their vigorous health secure. For this reason they were more desirable to their husbands and more lovable, for they made not only their bodies but also their souls better and more virtuous.

So, you see, as Rebecca arrived in Abraham's country

sitting on the camel, before she came near, she looked up and saw Isaac, and jumped down from her camel. Do you see her strength? Do you see her vigor? She jumped down from the camel. The girls of those days had such strength along with chastity. "She said to the servant, 'Who is that man walking in the field?' The servant said, 'It is my master.' So she took her veil and covered herself."[40] See how her chastity is shown by everything she did, how modest and worthy of respect she was. "So Isaac took Rebecca, and she became his wife, and he loved her. So Isaac was comforted after the death of Sarah his mother."[41] There is a purpose in saying that Isaac loved Rebecca and was comforted after the death of Sarah his mother. The story is told to teach you the reasons for his attraction and love, the good qualities which his wife brought with her from her home. Who would not have loved such a woman, so virtuous, so beautiful, so hospitable, generous, and kind, so brave in her soul and vigorous in her body?

I have told this story not only for you to hear, not only for you to praise, but also for you to emulate. You fathers, imitate the foresight of Abraham, the care which he used to find an unaffected woman for Isaac's wife. He did not look for money, for high birth, for beauty of body, or anything else but nobility of soul. You mothers, bring up your daughters as Rebecca was brought up. You bridegrooms who are about to marry girls like Rebecca, celebrate your weddings with as much decorum as Isaac did. Banish dancing, laughter, shameful speeches, the music of pipes and flutes, and all the devil's show. Instead you must beseech God to preside over all that is done. If we manage our families in this way, there will never be divorce, suspicion of adultery, occasion for jealousy, battles, or

---

[40]Gen 24:65.
[41]Gen 24:67.

strife. Rather we shall enjoy great tranquillity and great harmony. When we have these, the other virtues will undoubtedly follow. Just as, when a wife is at odds with her husband, nothing will be healthy in the household, even if all other affairs are flowing with the current; so when the wife is in harmony and peace with her husband, nothing will be unpleasant, even if innumerable storms arise every day. If marriages are begun in this way, we will be able to raise our children to virtue with great ease. When the mother is so decorous and chaste and endowed with every virtue, she will undoubtedly be able to attract her husband and subject him to love for her. When she has caught him, she will keep him willingly helping her in the care of the children, and so she will bring God's providence to join in this same care. When He takes a part in this good management of the household, when He trains the souls of the children, nothing at all will be unpleasant. The affairs of the household will go well when its rulers are so well disposed. In this way each man together with his household (I mean his wife, children, and servants) will be able to finish the course of this life without fear and to enter the kingdom of heaven: which may we all attain, by the grace and love of our Lord Jesus Christ, with whom to the Father be glory and might, together with the holy and life-giving Spirit, now and ever and unto ages of ages. Amen.